# GREEK GENIUS
# AND OTHER ESSAYS

# GREEK GENIUS
## AND OTHER ESSAYS

BY

JOHN JAY CHAPMAN

*Essay Index Reprint Series*

BOOKS FOR LIBRARIES PRESS, INC.

FREEPORT, NEW YORK

First Published 1915
First Reprinting in this Series 1967
Second Reprinting 1969

STANDARD BOOK NUMBER:

8369-0289-0


LIBRARY OF CONGRESS CATALOG CARD NUMBER:

67-23192


PRINTED IN THE UNITED STATES OF AMERICA

# CONTENTS

# CONTENTS

# I
## EURIPIDES AND THE
## GREEK GENIUS

# I

## INTRODUCTION

THE teasing perfection of Greek Literature will perhaps excite the world
long after modern literature is forgotten.
Shakespeare may come to his end and lie
down among the Egyptians, but Homer will
endure forever. We hate to imagine such
an outcome, because, while we love Shakespeare, we regard the Greek classics merely
with an overwhelmed astonishment. But
the fact is that Homer floats in the central
stream of History, Shakespeare in an eddy.
There is, too, a real difference between ancient and modern art, and the enduring
power may be on the side of antiquity.

The classics will always be the playthings
of humanity, because they are types of perfection, like crystals. They are pure intellect, like demonstrations in geometry.
Within their own limitations they are examples of miracle; and the modern world has
nothing to show that resembles them in the
least. As no builder has built like the

[ 3 ]

Greeks, so no writer has written like the
Greeks. In edge, in delicacy, in proportion,
in accuracy of effect, they are as marble to
our sandstone. The perfection of the Greek
vehicle is what attacks the mind of the modern man and gives him dreams.

What relation these dreams bear to Greek
feeling it is impossible to say,—probably a
very remote and grotesque relation. The
scholars who devote their enormous energies in a life-and-death struggle to understand the Greeks always arrive at states of
mind which are peculiarly modern. The same
thing may be said of the severest types of
Biblical scholar. David Friedrich Strauss, for
instance, gave his life to the study of Christ,
and, as a result, has left an admirable picture
of the German mind of 1850. Goethe, who
was on his guard if ever a man could be, has
still been a little deceived in thinking that
the classic spirit could be recovered. He has
left imitations of Greek literature which are
admirable in themselves, and rank among
his most characteristic works, yet which
bear small resemblance to the originals. The
same may be said of Milton and of Racine.
The Greeks seem to have used their material,
their myths and ideas, with such supernal
intellect that they leave this material un-

touched for the next comer. Their gods persist, their mythology is yours and mine. We accept the toys,—the whole babyhouse which has come down to us: we walk in and build our own dramas with their blocks.

What a man thinks of influences him, though he chance to know little about it; and the power which the ancient world has exerted over the modern has not been shown in proportion to the knowledge or scholarship of the modern thinker, but in proportion to his natural force. The Greek tradition, the Greek idea became an element in all subsequent life; and one can no more dig it out and isolate it than one can dig out or isolate a property of the blood. We do not know exactly how much we owe to the Greeks. Keats was inspired by the very idea of them. They were an obsession to Dante, who knew not the language. Their achievements have been pressing in upon the mind of Europe, and enveloping it with an atmospheric appeal, ever since the Dark Ages.

Of late years we have come to think of all subjects as mere departments of science, and we are almost ready to hand over Greece to the specialist. We assume that scholars will work out the history of art. But it is not the right of the learned and scholarly only, to be

influenced by the Greeks, but also of those
persons who know no Greek. Greek influence is too universal an inheritance to be
entrusted to scholars, and the specialist is the
very last man who can understand it. In
order to obtain a diagnosis on Greek influence one would have to seek out a sort of
specialist on Humanity-at-large.

## II

### FALSE GUIDES

SINCE we cannot find any inspired
teacher to lay before us the secrets of
Greek influence, the next best thing would
be to go directly to the Greeks themselves,
and to study their works freshly, almost innocently. But to do this is not easy. The
very Greek texts themselves have been established through modern research, and the
foot-notes are the essence of modernity.

The rushing modern world passes like an
express train; as it goes, it holds up a mirror
to the classic world,—a mirror ever chang-
ing and ever false. For upon the face of the
mirror rests the lens of fleeting fashion. We
can no more walk straight to the Greeks than
we can walk straight to the moon. In
America the natural road to the classics lies
through the introductions of German and
English scholarship. We are met, as it
were, on the threshold of Greece by guides
who address us confidently in two very dis-

[ 7 ]

similar modern idioms, and who overwhelm us with complacent and voluble instructions. According to these men we have nothing to do but listen to them, if we would understand Greece.

Before entering upon the subject of Greece, let us cast a preliminary and disillusioning glance upon our two guides, the German and the Briton. Let us look once at each of them with an intelligent curiosity, so that we may understand what manner of men they are, and can make allowances in receiving the valuable and voluble assistance which they keep whispering into our ears throughout the tour. The guides are indispensable; but this need not prevent us from studying their temperaments. If it be true that modern scholarship acts as a lens through which the classics are to be viewed, we can never hope to get rid of all the distortions; but we may make scientific allowances, and may correct results. We may consider certain social laws of refraction; for example, spectacles, beer, sausages. We may regard the variations of the compass due to certain local customs, namely: the Anglican communion, School honour, Pears' soap. In all this we sin not, but pursue intellectual methods.

# EURIPIDES AND GREEK GENIUS

The case of Germany illustrates the laws of refraction very pleasantly. The extraordinary lenses which were made there in the nineteenth century are famous now, and will remain as curiosities hereafter. During the last century, Learning won the day in Germany to an extent never before known in history. It became an unwritten law of the land that none but learned men should be allowed to play with pebbles. If a man had been through the mill of the Doctorate, however, he received a certificate as a dreamer. The passion which mankind has for using its imagination could thus be gratified only by men who *had been* brilliant scholars. The result was a race of monsters, of whom Nietzsche is the greatest.

The early social life of these men was contracted. They learned all they knew while sitting on a bench. The classroom was their road to glory. They were aware that they could not be allowed to go out and play in the open until they had learned their lessons thoroughly; they therefore became prize boys. When the great freedom was at last conferred upon them, they roamed through Greek mythology, and all other mythologies, and erected labyrinths in which the passions of childhood may be seen gambolling with the discoveries of adult miseducation. The gravity with which the pundits treated each other extended to the rest of the world, because, in the first place, they were more learned than any one else, and in the second, several of them were men of genius. The "finds" of modern archæology have passed through the hands of these men, and have received from them the labels of current classification.

After all, these pundits resemble their predecessors in learning. Scholarship is always a specialised matter, and it must be learned as we learn a game. Scholarship always wears the parade of finality, and yet suffers changes like the moon. These particular scholars are merely scholars. Their errors are only the errors of scholarship, due, for the most part, to extravagance and to ambition. A new idea about Hellas meant a new reputation. In default of such an idea a man's career is *manquée;* he is not an intellectual. After discounting ambition, we have left still another cause for distrusting the labours of the German professors. This distrust arises from a peep into the social surroundings of the caste. Here is a great authority on the open-air life of the Greeks: he knows all about Hellenic sport.

# EURIPIDES AND GREEK GENIUS

Here is another who understands the brilliant social life of Attica: he has written the best book upon Athenian conversation and the market-place. Here is still a third: he has reconstructed Greek religion: at last we know! All these miracles of learning have been accomplished in the library,—without athletics, without conversation, without religion.

When I think of Greek civilisation, of the swarming, thieving, clever, gleaming-eyed Greeks, of the Bay of Salamis, and of the Hermes of Praxiteles,—and then cast my eyes on the Greatest Authority, my guide, my Teuton master, with his barbarian babble and his ham-bone and his self-importance, I begin to wonder whether I cannot somehow get rid of the man and leave him behind. Alas, we cannot do that; we can only remember his traits.

Our British mentors, who flank the German scholars as we move gently forward toward Greek feeling, form so complete a contrast to the Teutons that we hardly believe that *both* kinds can represent genuine scholarship. The Britons are gentlemen, afternoon callers, who eat small cakes, row on the Thames, and are all for morality. They are men of letters. They write in

prose and in verse, and belong to the æsthetic fraternity. They, like the Teutons,
are attached to institutions of learning,
namely, to Oxford and Cambridge. They
resemble the Germans, however, in but a
single trait,—the conviction that they understand Greece.

The thesis of the British belle-lettrists, to
which they devote their energies, might be
stated thus: British culture includes Greek
culture. They are very modern, very English, very sentimental, these British scholars.
While the German doctors use Greek as
a stalking-horse for Teutonic psychology,
these English gentlemen use it as a dress-
maker's model upon which they exhibit
home-made English lyrics and British stock
morality. The lesson which Browning sees
in *Alcestis* is the same that he gave us in
*James Lee's Wife.* Browning's appeal is
always the appeal to robust feeling as the
salvation of the world. Gilbert Murray, on
the other hand, sheds a sad, clinging, Tenny-
sonian morality over Dionysus. Jowett is
happy to announce that Plato is theologically
sound, and gives him a ticket-of-leave to
walk anywhere in England. Swinburne
clings to that belief in sentiment which
marks the Victorian era, but Swinburne

finds the key to life in unrestraint instead of in restraint.

There is a whole school of limp Grecism in England, which has grown up out of Keats' Grecian urn, and which is now buttressed with philosophy and adorned with scholarship; and no doubt it does bear some sort of relation to Greece and to Greek life. But this Anglican Grecism has the quality which all modern British art exhibits,—the very quality which the Greeks could not abide,—it is tinged with *excess*. The Briton likes strong flavours. He likes them in his tea, in his port wine, in his concert-hall songs, in his pictures of home and farm life. He likes something unmistakable, something with a smack that lets you know that the thing has arrived. In his literature he is the same. Dickens, Carlyle, Tennyson lay it on thick with sentiment. Keats drips with aromatic poetry, which has a wonder and a beauty of its own—and whose striking quality is *excess*. The scented, wholesale sweetness of the modern æsthetic school in England goes home to its admirers because it is easy art. Once enjoy a bit of it and you never forget it. It is always the same, the "old reliable," the Oxford brand, the true, safe, British, patriotic, moral, noble school

of verse; which exhibits the manners and
feelings of a gentleman, and has success
written in every trait of its physiognomy.

How this school of poetry invaded Greece
is part of the history of British expansion in
the nineteenth century. In the Victorian era
the Englishman brought cricket and morning prayers into South Africa. Robert
Browning established himself and his carpet-
bag in comfortable lodgings on the Acropo-
lis,—which he spells with a *k* to show his
intimate acquaintance with recent research.
It must be confessed that Robert Browning's
view of Greece never pleased, even in England. It was too obviously R. B. over again.
It was *Pippa* and *Bishop Blougram* with a
few pomegranate seeds and unexpected or-
thographies thrown in. The *Encyclopædia
Britannica* is against it, and suggests, wittily
enough, that one can hardly agree with
Browning that Heracles got drunk for the
purpose of keeping up *other* people's spirits.

So also Edward Fitzgerald was never
taken seriously by the English; but this was
for another reason. His translations are the
best transcriptions from the Greek ever done
by this British school; but Fitzgerald never
took himself seriously. I believe that if he
had only been ambitious, and had belonged

to the academic classes,—like Jowett for instance,—he could have got Oxford behind him, and we should all have been obliged to regard him as a great apostle of Hellenism. But he was a poor-spirited sort of man, and never worked up his lead.

Matthew Arnold, on the other hand, began the serious profession of being a Grecian. He took it up when there was nothing in it, and he developed a little sect of his own, out of which later came Swinburne and Gilbert Murray, each of whom is the true British article. While Swinburne is by far the greater poet, Murray is by far the more important of the two from the ethnological point of view. Murray was the first man to talk boldly about God, and to introduce his name into all Greek myths, using it as a fair translation of any Greek thought. There is a danger in this boldness. The reader's attention becomes hypnotised with wondering in what manner God is to be introduced into the next verse. The reader becomes so concerned about Mr. Murray's religious obsessions that he forgets the Greek altogether and remembers only Shakespeare's hostess in her distress over the dying Falstaff: "Now I, to comfort him, bid him 'a should not think of God,—I hoped there was no need to trouble himself with any such thoughts yet."

Murray and Arnold are twins in ethical endeavour. I think that it was Arnold who first told the British that Greece was noted for melancholy and for longings. He told them that chastity, temperance, nudity, and a wealth of moral rhetoric marked the young man of the Periclean period. Even good old Dean Plumptre has put this young man into his prefaces. Swinburne added the hymeneal note,—the poetic nature-view, —of which the following may serve as an example :—

"And the trees in their season brought
        forth and were kindled anew
By the warmth of the mixture of mar-
        riage, the child-bearing dew."

There is hardly a page in Swinburne's Hellenising verse that does not blossom with Hymen. The passages would be well suited for use in the public schools of to-day where sex-knowledge in its poetic aspects is beginning to be judiciously introduced.

This contribution of Swinburne's,—the hymeneal touch,—and Murray's discovery that the word God could be introduced with effect anywhere, went like wildfire over England. They are characteristic of the latest phase of Anglo-Grecism.

Gilbert Murray has, in late years, had the field to himself. He stands as the head and front of Greek culture in England. It is he, more than any one else, who is the figure-head of dramatic poetry in England to-day; and, as such, his influence must be met, and, as it were, passed through, by the American student who is studying the Greek classics. It is then no accident that a chapter at the end of this essay is devoted to Gilbert Murray. In studying the vagaries of the Anglo-Grecian school, it is necessary to take Greek itself as a central objective, and then super-pose the Anglican transcriptions on top of the original.

## III

### THE *ALCESTIS*

IN this and the following chapter two plays of Euripides, the *Alcestis* and the *Bacchantes,* are examined as dispassionately as may be for the purpose of gaining some insight into the Greek mind. The *Alcestis* is plain sailing, and no one will quarrel very seriously as to its nature. The *Bacchantes,* on the other hand, is the most tousled bit of all Greek literature. It is the happy hunting-ground of all religious interpretations, and no two scholars agree with certainty about its meaning. Ancient religion is of all subjects in the world the most difficult. Every religion, even at the time it was in progress, was always completely misunderstood, and the misconceptions have increased with the ages. They multiply with every monument that is unearthed. If the Eleusinian mysteries were going at full blast to-day, so that we could attend them, as we do the play at Oberammergau, their interpretation would still present difficulties.

[19]

GREEK GENIUS

Mommsen and Rhode would disagree. And ten thousand years from now, when nothing survives except a line out of St. John's Gospel and a tablet stating that Meyer played the part of Christ for three successive decades, many authoritative books will be written about Oberammergau, and reputations will be made over it. Anything which we approach as religion becomes a nightmare of suggestion, and hales us hither and thither with thoughts beyond the reaches of the soul.

The *Alcestis* and the *Bacchantes* are, in this paper, approached with the idea that they are *plays*. This seems not to have been done often enough with Greek plays. They are regarded as examples of the sublime, as forms of philosophic thought, as moral essays, as poems, even as illustrations of dramatic law, and they are unquestionably all of these things. But they were primarily plays, —intended to pass the time and exhilarate the emotions. They came into being as plays, and their form and make-up can best be understood by a study of the dramatic business in them. They became poems and philosophy incidentally, and afterwards: they were born as plays. A playwright is always an entertainer, and unless his desire to hold his audience overpoweringly predominates he will never be a success. It is probable that even with Æschylus—who stands *hors ligne* as the only playwright in history who was really in earnest about morality—we should have to confess that his passion as a dramatic artist came *first*. He held his audiences by strokes of tremendous dramatic novelty. Both the stage traditions and the plays themselves bear this out. The fact is that it is not easy to keep people sitting in a theatre; and unless the idea of holding their attention predominates with the author, they will walk out, and he will not be able to deliver the rest of his story.

In the grosser forms of dramatic amusement—for example, where a bicycle acrobat is followed by a comic song—we are not compelled to find any philosophic depth of idea in the sequence. But in dealing with works of great and refined dramatic genius like the *Tempest,* or the *Bacchantes,* where the emotions played upon are subtly interwoven, there will always be found certain minds which remain unsatisfied with the work of art itself, but must have it explained. Even Beethoven's sonatas have been supplied with philosophic addenda,—statements of their meaning. We know how much Shakespeare's intentions used to puzzle the Germans. Men feel that somewhere at the back of their own consciousness there is a philosophy or a religion with which the arts have some relation. In so far as these affinities are touched upon in a manner that leaves them mysteries, we have good criticism; but when people dogmatise about them, we have bad criticism. In the meantime the great artist goes his way. His own problems are enough for him.

The early critics were puzzled to classify the *Alcestis,* and no wonder, for it contains many varieties of dramatic writing. For this very reason it is a good play to take as a sample of Greek spirit and Greek workmanship. It is a little Greek cosmos, and it happens to depict a side of Greek thought which is sympathetic to modern sentiment, so that we seem to be at home in its atmosphere. The *Alcestis* is thought to be in a class by itself. And yet, under close examination, every Greek play falls into a class by itself (there are only about forty-five of them in all), and the maker of each was more concerned with the dramatic experiment upon which he found himself launched than he was with any formal classification which posterity might assign to his play.

# EURIPIDES AND GREEK GENIUS

In the *Alcestis* Euripides made one of the best plays in the world, full of true pathos, full of jovial humour, both of which sometimes verge upon the burlesque. The happy ending is understood from the start, and none of the grief is painful. Alcestis herself is the goodwife of Greek household myth, who is ready to die for her husband. To this play the *bourgeois* takes his half-grown family. He rejoices when he hears that it is to be given. The absurdities of the fairy-tale are accepted simply. Heracles has his club, Death his sword, Apollo his lyre. The women wail, Admetus whines; there is buffoonery, there are tears, there is wit, there is conventional wrangling, and that word-chopping so dear to the Mediterranean theatre, which exists in all classic drama and survives in the Punch and Judy show of to-day. And there is the charming return of Heracles with the veiled lady whom he presents to Admetus as a slave for safe-keeping, whom Admetus refuses to receive for conventional reasons, but whom every child in the audience feels to be the real Alcestis, even before Heracles unveils her and gives her back into her husband's bosom with speeches on both sides that are like the closing music of a dream.

# GREEK GENIUS

The audience disperses at the close, feeling that it has spent a happy hour. No sonata of Mozart is more completely beautiful than the *Alcestis*. No comedy of Shakespeare approaches it in perfection. The merit of the piece lies not in any special idea it conveys, but entirely in the manner in which everything is carried out.

At the risk of fatiguing the reader I must give a rapid summary of the *Alcestis,* so as to show some aspects of the play from a purely dramatic point of view, as well as to consider what the Greek theatre at large was like.

At the opening of the play Apollo appears upon the steps of the palace of Admetus and explains that he is Apollo and that the palace is the palace. It appears that out of regard for Admetus, in whose house he had formerly lived, Apollo has agreed with Death to lengthen Admetus' life if a substitute can be found. The fatal day has arrived, but no one is willing to die in place of Admetus, except his wife, Alcestis, who now lies, *in articulo mortis,* within the palace. Apollo is about to leave, so as to escape the presence of anything so defiling as a dead body, when Death stalks upon the scene, and the two have a most senseless bout of word-whack-

[24]

ing and mutual defiance, somewhat in the
style of Herod and Pilate in an old market-
place comedy. During this bout the very
simple situation of the plot becomes defi-
nitely fixed in the mind of the top gallery.
These two figures, Death and Apollo, stand
like huge, crude images at the portal of the
play. They are grotesque, and are intended
to be so. One must remember that everything in the Greek theatre had to be larger
than life as well as symbolic in character.
Inasmuch as the physical scale of the setting
is enlarged, the ideas themselves must be
simplified and exaggerated. The masked
characters on the Greek stage must always
be thought of as *great marionettes,* rather
than as men. Their language will always be
wrong, and often becomes intolerable if
imagined as coming from the mouths of
actors in a small theatre. In a great Greek
theatre the costume and dialogue formed a
sort of sign-language of conventional exaggeration. Realism is never in question: the
fact that the whole affair is a fiction is always held in mind by the Greek. The Greek
does not do this on purpose; he cannot help
doing it. The whole play is to him merely
the image of an idea cast upon the screen of
the imagination. So then, Death and Apollo

strike at each other with verbal truncheons, till Apollo, becoming exasperated, prophesies that he is going to triumph in the end, because Heracles is to appear and save the situation. Thus ends the prologue. Death goes into the palace to execute his office upon Alcestis; Apollo departs in another direction.

The chorus of women wailers now begin to creep in, in a furtive, distributive manner, and to ask questions of each other as to whether Alcestis is really dead yet. "Ah, what a woman! No one ever was like her! . . . How can we save her now? . . . Not even a voyage to Libya will recover her now! . . . Ah me, ah me! . . . But is she really laid out yet? I don't see the signs of mourning on the house. . . . O Admetus, you don't know yet how great your loss is!" etc., etc. This chorus gives a *pianissimo* introduction to that wholesale blubbering and wailing, the luxurious smiting and rending and sobbing of conventional grief, which will, a little later, roll from the orchestra across the delighted and gloating audience. A Greek play is an opera and its effects are operatic. The iterations of idea, which the great size of the theatre made necessary, were accomplished through the questionings and comments of the Chorus, which acted as a sounding-board. The Chorus retards the action and keeps magnifying the reverberations of thought and sending them to every part of the auditorium.

The grieving women are now confronted by a maid-servant, who enters from the central doors and describes the last moments of Alcestis. No picture was ever framed with more art than this of Alcestis. It is gigantic in scale, but the exaggerations are so managed that five thousand people can enjoy it as well as if it were a miniature held in their hands. The servant describes the last hours of her mistress: "When she perceived that the destined day was come, she washed her fair skin with water from the river; and having taken from her closet of cedar vesture and ornaments, she attired herself becomingly; and standing before the altar, she prayed: 'O mistress, since I go beneath the earth, adoring thee for the last time, I will beseech thee to protect my orphan children, and to the one join a loving wife, and to the other, a noble husband: nor, as their mother perishes, let my children untimely die, but happy in their paternal country let them complete a joyful life.' And then to all the altars which are in the house of Admetus she went, and crowned them, and prayed, tearing the leaves from off the myrtle boughs, tearless, without a groan; nor did the approaching evil change the natural beauty of her skin. And then rushing to her chamber and her bed, there indeed she wept and spoke thus: 'O bridal bed, whereon I loosed my virgin zone with this man, for whom I die, farewell! For I hate thee not; but me alone hast thou lost; for dreading to betray thee and my husband, I die; but thee some other woman will possess, more chaste there cannot be, but perchance more fortunate.' And falling on it she kissed it; and all the bed was bathed with the flood that issued from her eyes. . . . And her children, hanging on the garments of their mother, wept; but she, taking them in her arms, embraced them, first one, and then the other, as about to die. And all the domestics wept throughout the house, bewailing their mistress, but she stretched out her right hand to each, and there was none so mean but she addressed him, and was answered in return. Such are the woes of the house of Admetus. And had he died indeed, he would have perished; but now that he has escaped death, he has grief to that degree which he will never forget."

# EURIPIDES AND GREEK GENIUS

The picture is exquisite and impersonal. The pose, supplied by the legend, has been studied with care. Each fold in the robe is significant. The character is a mere resultant from the accurate following of the fable. Here we have the touch of "Euripides the Human, with his droppings of warm tears," as Mrs. Browning called him. Yet nothing could be further from the truth than to imagine that Euripides himself wept while penning this scene or any other. Mrs. Browning's line leaves us a little too much in doubt as to just who is doing the weeping. The Greek artist does not weep, and Euripides the least of all men. Precisely the same method is pursued by him in depicting Admetus. This equivocal character is provided by the plot. Admetus must exact his wife's sacrifice, and yet moan mightily. His situation is ridiculous, and yet it is insisted upon with stoical rigour by Euripides, who saws the character out of the board, and sticks it up in all its crudity and self-contradiction; and lo, instead of becoming a blemish, it becomes a foil and adds lustre to the play.

"Admetus," continues the maid-servant, "is at this moment holding his dying wife in his arms, and is beseeching her not to betray

him, not to forsake him,—impracticable re-
quests." Again the Chorus in antiphonal
crescendo lash themselves to a climax of
professional woe, such as all ancient peoples
indulged in, and such as may be heard in any
Hebrew cemetery at the present day. Curiously enough, the Greek phrases here give
forth an Hebraic clang. "Cry aloud, wail,
O land of Pheræ! Never, never will I say
that marriage brings more joy than grief,"
etc.

The opera now begins in earnest. Alcestis
enters, assisted by Admetus. Two children,
a boy and a girl, cling to her skirts. A duet
ensues,—an actual duet with musical accompaniment. Both Alcestis and Admetus
burst into song at the very top of passionate
utterance:

"*Alcestis.* O sun-god, lamp of day! O scud-
ding clouds that dance along the sky!
*Admetus.* He sees thee and me also,—two
sufferers who have done nothing worthy
of death.
*Alcestis.* O Earth! O sheltering roof! and
ye chambers of my maidenhood," etc.

She sees the skiff of Charon; she feels the
hand of death clutching her. Her limbs are

giving way, the halls of Hades loom over her: she calls wildly to her children. Admetus continues to put in his "me too" in the proper tenor voice. The scene is like the end of the first act of grand opera. Both characters are at the footlights, singing their uttermost. The tenor is clutching the lady's wrist and she is straining towards the stars.

But a Greek play was never divided into acts, and so, when the spasm is over, Alcestis collects herself for her great testamentary speech. Here is another masterpiece of the pathetic, which rehearses the entire situation. Alcestis begs Admetus not to marry again, for fear lest a stepmother should maltreat the children. Admetus consents, and proceeds to lift a long-drawn tragic wail, precisely as if he were a moral hero. He will wear mourning, not for a year, but all his life; he will forego music and company. He will have an image made by cunning artists, and place it in his bed, and upon this he will cast himself in paroxysms of unavailing grief.

Admetus' character is that of a wooden nut-cracker; and we feel a note of irony, a note almost of humour, when these exalted sentiments flow from him. It is true that any diminution of the size of the theatre would tinge Admetus' speeches here with burlesque. But as they stand they are not burlesque. The exaggeration is precisely in keeping with the exaggeration of Alcestis herself. The merit of the whole lies in the subtlety with which the scale of values is adhered to. These edges and curvatures, taken together, are what cast the image on the air. Euripides is merely setting the legend upon the stage in an effective way, so that a child or a peasant can enjoy it.

When Admetus has made an end of his threnody, there follows a final duet in prose, —at the end of which Alcestis dies. The boy then flings himself upon his mother's body, music sounds and the voice of a hidden singer behind the scenes gives the lyric: "Hear me, hear me, mother, I implore thee!" Alcestis' body is borne into the palace, followed by Admetus and the children; and the Chorus raises a quiet, conventional, soothing and very beautiful hymn: "Daughter of Pelias, be thine a happy life in the sunless home of Hades' halls! Of thee the Muses' votaries shall sing on the seven-stringed mountain shell in hymns without a harp." Nothing could be more satisfying than the simple subsidence of this whole sad episode: the closing of the palace doors, the peaceful music; and thereupon—what next follows —the unexpected, sudden appearance of Heracles, ignorant, boorish, and good-hearted,—radiant Heracles, the demigod and friend to man. He falls into chat with the Chorus about a mission which he has undertaken into Thessaly, and about the dangers of his life in a general way. Here we have a plunge from tragedy into joyful comedy of a Shakespearian kind,—a transition very unusual in Greek plays. Greek drama is full of variety, and the tints of its clouds change at every moment; but the gradations are generally slight. These extremes in the *Alcestis* were, no doubt, what puzzled the critics to classify the play. A talk now ensues between Heracles and the Chorus, which resembles a conversation between a schoolboy and the coachman. It touches on hard adventures, fire-breathing steeds, heroic strife. Then re-enter Admetus, this time as the host who has heard that his old friend is at the door. The scene is buskined, of course; but the substance of it is the meeting of hearty comrades, club men, no longer young:

"My dear fellow! how are you? Quite well, I trust?"

"I should hope so! And you, old man?"

GREEK GENIUS

"You stay, of course?"

"So it seems."

"Bravo! Your room is ready."

"But how about all this mourning? Not one of the family, I hope?"

"Yes, no,—a relative, yet no relation. I 'll tell you."

"It is impossible, you know, for me to come in and be entertained by you while the mourning is going on."

"Your room is on the other side of the house. A woman, my dear boy,—a sort of dependent. (*To the servants.*) Here, some of you fellows, show Heracles his room and be quick about it!"

This burly Admetus, it must be observed, has no relation to the whining Admetus of the first act. No attempt is made to connect them. There is no such thing in a Greek play as what we to-day should call character-drawing. The artist is always merely dressing a stock character, or giving his own version of a well-known tale. The problem is to illustrate the legend; the characters must look after themselves; they come out right if the legend is right. If the legend, as in this case, cracks up a character into separate personalities, nobody objects; it is all the more entertaining. After all, the progress of almost every good plot, whether ancient or modern, depends upon the fact that somebody acts in a very unlikely way. The modern writer wastes his talents in toiling at this weak place. The ancient accepts it cheerfully. This is one of the blessings of having legend as a foundation for fiction. The absurdities are the very points that no one will question.

Admetus enters the palace, and the Chorus sings a lyric in praise of the hospitality of his house, "where Pythian Apollo, the sweet harper, once deigned to make his home, while spotted lynxes couched amid the sheep in joy to hear his melodies,—since which time riches and blessings are poured upon one who welcomes the guest, though his eyes are wet with tears; and at my heart sits the belief that heaven's servant will be blessed."

There next ensues a most amusing and original scene which Euripides throws in as a make-weight on the comic side. The corpse of Alcestis is borne forth upon a bier; Admetus comes with it; a train is formed to accompany the corpse to the pyre. The small procession is, however, confronted by another small procession which appears from the wings: Pheres, the father of Admetus, has come with his conventional condolences

and ritual gifts for the dead, the gifts being
borne by servants. We had forgotten
Pheres, though, from time to time, someone
on the stage had spoken ill of him because
of his refusal to die for his son. Pheres
himself is entirely unconscious of the odium
in which he stands, and he makes a proper
speech. He is met by a torrent of abuse
from Admetus. The Chorus protests against
the indecency of this public quarrel; but
Pheres though old is not feeble, and defends
himself with scorching power. Again the
Chorus is shocked; and a line-for-line,
hammer-and-tongs Billingsgate follows, of
the sort dear to the Athenian audience. The
protagonists finally separate, leaving shafts
in the air: each has his cortège behind him
as he hurls back insults: "Go bury thy victim with the hand that murdered her!" "I
disown thy paternal hearth, and if need be, I
will proclaim it by heralds!"

This scene is intolerable if taken seriously;
but is delightful if we bear in mind while
reading it the so-called "New Comedy" of
the Greeks, which survives only in the form
of the Roman imitations. This New Comedy was a comedy of manners, and came to
blossom a couple of generations later than
Aristophanes. On its stage fathers and

sons, masters and servants, live in a hurly-burly of rapid-fire talk. The modern Italian name for this sort of scene is *botta e risposta*. The roots of the New Comedy undoubtedly extended back into classic drama, and it is thus quite natural that Euripides should have written a scene that must be read by the light of Plautus.

The next scene is frankly comic, and in the very greatest manner. The arrival of Heracles at the house of mourning, and his innocent, gluttonous feasting while the dead body lies in the next room, is one of the most vigorous ideas in Greek mythology, and is exactly fitted for the stage. First comes a servant's description of Heracles' revelry and wassailing, and next enter Heracles himself, in his cups, and crowned with myrtle. He gives the speech which might be called "Heracles' advice to servants":

"Ho, you there! What scowling, what pomposity! Is that the way to treat a guest? Why don't you be polite? But what does one like you know about life? Come here; listen to me. All must die, and no man knows if he shall see the morrow's dawn. Fate walks darkling, and cannot be caught with all your cleverness. Now list, learn, be wise by me. What of it all then, I say?

What of it all? Why, drink and bless thyself with the day. Dismiss all else into the realm of chance. Second, avoid chastity; for Venus is a goddess. As for the rest, trust one that knows: for I am right about this! What, man! Dismiss thy bad temper; crown thy brows, and smooth them out, too. The splash of the wine will cure thee! Leave the dead for dead, and get wisdom; for the knotted forehead of piety never knew a life that was life at all, but only pure misery."

Heracles' attack on the servant naturally leads to an explanation of the cause of mourning in the house, and to the immediate sobering up of Heracles himself. His soliloquy follows,—the solemn address in which he declares his intention of lying in wait for Death at the tomb of Alcestis, of overcoming the monster with his mighty hands, and of restoring the woman to the noble host who had concealed his sorrow rather than drive the guest from the door. Heracles goes off to watch by the tomb, and immediately enter Admetus.

We are now prepared to enjoy a little more wailing and lyrical business. The return to the empty house is celebrated in antiphony between the Chorus and Admetus. They begin *piano:*

[38]

"Home again! Alas, what have you not suffered! Ah me, a noble wife buried!"

"Ah, you touch the wound! How can I bear to see my own roof-tree! I envy the dead. I envy the childless!"

"You are not the first."

"Why did you prevent me from leaping into the tomb?"

"It must be borne."

"O to contrast this day with the hour when I entered this house,—with the marriage torch, and the shout of banqueting; but now, grave-clothes for wedding garments, and woe for hymns. The empty couch, the chairs she sat in,—the desolation of it drives me out!"

This scene gives the poet a new opportunity, and again "Euripides the Human" works up all possible suggestions of the pathetic with cunning hand. There is, perhaps, a touch of virtuosity in the appeal. One feels that one is being played upon: the hand is almost too cunning. Yet who can regret its skill? The wooden Admetus of the earlier part and the burly clubman Admetus of the central scene are here succeeded by a romantic Admetus,—a throstle-throated widower, who mourns his lost saint. The very dust on the furniture smites the wretch,

[39]

till he declares in true penitence that he
wishes he had not made the bargain. "This
—this is worse than death!"

No one can deny the dramatic beauty of
Admetus' grief in this scene. The beauty is
just the part that gets lost in transcription.
Here is a speech comparable to one of the
great arias in an Italian opera. When Euripides chooses to be sweet, there is hardly
anything like his sweetness in all literature.
The lines have a thrill like the appeal of a
tenor voice. We can and ought to weep, not
bitterly but happily, as the Italian matron
does at the melodrama, murmuring, *"E
bello! E bello!"*

When, shortly after this, Heracles returns
with the veiled lady, whom he says he has
won in an open-to-all prize contest, he finds
Admetus extremely unwilling to take her in;
and from this point to the end of the play,
which is not far distant, we have one of
those stage situations of the perfect comedy,
—touching, gay, charming and obvious,—
the thing the stage exists for, the only danger being lest the lucky playwright shall drag
it out and overdo it; which Euripides does
not. Heracles beseeches Admetus to harbour
the lady for a season, as a special and personal favour. Admetus is divided between

his reverence for the god and his regard for appearances. He is, in fact, caught between his own two crack virtues—hospitality and professional widowhood. At last he gives way and the play closes quietly and quickly with half a dozen stock lines from the Chorus.

It is clear at a glance that the *Alcestis* belongs to an epoch of extreme sophistication. Everything has been thought out and polished; every ornament is a poem. If a character has to give five words of explanation or of prayer, it is done in silver. The tone is all the tone of cultivated society, the appeal is an appeal to the refined, casuistical intelligence. The smile of Voltaire is all through Greek literature; and it was not until the age of Louis XIV, or the Regency, that the modern world was again to know a refinement and a sophistication which recall the Greek work. Now, in one word, this subtlety which pleases us in matters of sentiment is the very thing that separates us from the Greek upon the profoundest questions of philosophy. Where religious or metaphysical truth is touched upon, either Greek sophistication carries us off our feet with a rapture which has no true relation to the subject, or else we are offended by it. We do not understand sophistication. The Greek has pushed æsthetic analysis further than the modern can bear. We follow well enough through the light issues, but when the deeper questions are reached we lose our footing. At this point the modern cries out in applause, "Religion, philosophy, pure feeling, the soul!"—He cries out, "Mystic cult, Asiatic influence, Nature worship,— deep things over there!"—Or else he cries, "What amazing cruelty, what cynicism!" And yet it is none of these things, but only the artistic perfection of the work which is moving us. We are the victims of clever stage management.

The cruder intelligence is ever compelled to regard the man of complex mind as a priest or as a demon. The child, for instance, asks about the character in a story, "But is he a good man or a bad man, papa?" The child must have a moral explanation of anything which is beyond his æsthetic comprehension. So also does the modern intelligence question the Greek.

The matter is complicated by yet another element,—namely, stage convention. Our modern stage is so different from the classic stage that we are bad judges of the Greek playwright's intentions. The quarrels which

arise as to allegorical or secondary meanings
in a work of art are generally connected
with some unfamiliar feature of its setting.
A great light is thrown upon any work of art
when we show how its form came into being,
and thus explain its primary meaning. Such
an exposition of the primary or apparent
meaning is often sufficient to put all secondary meanings out of court. For instance : It is, as we know, the Germans who
have found in Shakespeare a coherent philosophic intention. They think that he wrote
plays for the purpose of stating metaphysical truths. The Englishman does not
believe this, because the Englishman is familiar with that old English stage work. He
knows its traditions, its preoccupation with
story-telling, its mundane character, its
obliviousness to the sort of thing that Germany has in mind. The Englishman knows
the conventions of his own stage, and this
protects him from finding mares'-nests in
Shakespeare. Again, Shakespeare's son-
nets used to be a favourite field for mystical
exegesis, till Sir Sidney Lee explained their
form by reference to the sixteenth-century
sonnet literature of the Continent. This put
to flight many theories.

In other words, the appeal to convention

is the first duty of the scholar. But, unfortunately, in regard to the conventions of the Classic Stage, the moderns are all in the dark. Nothing like that stage exists to-day. We are obliged to make guesses as to its intentions, its humour, its relation to philosophy. If the classics had only possessed a cabinet-sized drama, like our own, we might have been at home there. But this giant talk, this megaphone-and-buskin method, offers us a problem in dynamics which staggers the imagination. All we can do is to tread lightly and guess without dogmatising. The typical Athenian, Euripides, was so much deeper-dyed in scepticism than any one since that day, that really no one has ever lived who could cross-question him,— let alone expound the meanings of his plays. In reading Euripides, we find ourselves ready to classify him at moments as a satirist, and at other moments as a man of feeling. Of course he was both. Sometimes he seems like a religious man, and again, like a charlatan. Of course he was neither. He was a playwright.

# IV

## THE *BACCHANTES*

THE coherence of any scheme of thought, even though it be coherence of thought shown in the operation of a loom for weaving carpets, excites in us a glow of admiration. We give to it almost a sentimental response of feeling. Thus the subtle Greek fire which lies hidden beneath the technical development of tragic themes upon the stage has always aroused a vague religiosity in modern poets, even when the themes dealt with were revolting or the stage effects were unknown or unappreciated by modern scholars. To Milton, to Goethe, to Swinburne, a Greek play is a feast of solemn declamation and of lyrical hymning, whose merit lies in the supreme beauty of its language and in the supposed moral exaltation of its ideas. Certainly the original Greek is characterised by great beauty of language; but a play is something more than a feast of song. A play is an exciting, varied, and deeply mov-

ing exhibition, where every word sparkles
with action, and every action with wit. Declamation and beauty are mere servants to
the plot and progress of the drama. In seeking to understand Greek plays we must forget Milton and think rather of Molière. We
must do all that we can to recover the vitality and the element of entertainment which
the original possessed. In this way alone
can we arrive at a guess as to what the work
meant to its first audiences.

I have, on an earlier page, likened a Greek
tragedy to an opera, because the opera is its
nearest living congener, and is a thing native and familiar to us all. Strictly speaking,
a Greek play was a musical drama; that is
to say, the spoken word, unaccompanied by
music, was the foundation and road-bed of
the drama: music was kept for the adorn-
ment of exciting passages, and for climaxes.
Such a division of territory between speech
and song is the most effective that can be
imagined on the stage; and it was an infinite loss to modern drama when the musi-
cians began to overrun the whole of the
libretto. The solemnity, the dead seriousness of spoken words,—to which the story
was constantly returning, and from which
it again leaped into music as from a spring-

board,—lent a sternness and a variety to Greek drama, which opera can never achieve until it shall adopt the Greek system as to the use of music. Half the power of the lyric is thrown away by making the whole text lyrical. We see in this disposition of the libretto by the Greeks an example of that mastery which is in all their artistic work. A Greek work of art is æsthetically correct: it is always right.

LET us now examine the *Bacchantes,* which is very unlike the *Alcestis* in externals; and yet very like it in metaphysical make-up and in stage technique. The indulgent reader will remember that it is impossible to give an account of a play without making that very sort of philosophic abstract which must always be false. A play is its own meaning, and no transcript will convey it. Any analysis must be regarded as a mere finger-post directing the reader towards the text.

The *Bacchantes* is as remarkable as anything in Hellenic art. The daring of it, the brilliancy of it, the outrageousness of it, the mockery it suggests and the gaiety with which it proceeds, its beauty and intellect,— are all subordinated to the success of the

whole as a dramatic show. No wonder that
Euripides did not publish the *Bacchantes*
during his lifetime. The natural power in
it was enough to hang any man; and Euripides was already a suspect. He had been
banished from Athens for some reason that
is not known, but which was perhaps connected with his treatment of religious topics
on the stage. We often commit witticisms
to the air, and then hold our breath and
hope for the best; and if the *Bacchantes* had
happened to come out at the moment of an
Athenian military defeat, the audacities of it
might have led to a tragedy in real life.

The *Bacchantes* is supposed by modern
scholars to be a mystical allegory. Both the
Germans and the Britons agree upon this.
There is, as Mr. Tyrrell says, "an ethical
contentment and speculative calm in the
play." I quote from the preface of Mr.
I. T. Beckwith's edition where Bernhardy
(*Griech. Ltg.*) is cited. Mr. Beckwith thus
describes the *Bacchantes:* "A play in which
faith celebrates its rites and unbelief is put
to shame, must, by reason of the seriousness
of its import and the lofty religious inspiration pervading the whole and manifesting
itself in many brilliant and profound utter-
ances, have attained great fame in antiquity.

It was much read, as the frequent citations and reminiscences in the Greek and Roman writers show, and was often cited." . . . "The choral odes follow the progress of the action more closely perhaps than in any other play of Euripides, expressing the emotions that accompany a devout faith as it passes from the most buoyant hopefulness, through a gradually darkening struggle, out again into a complete triumph."

Before leaving the serious part of the subject I cannot forbear to quote a few words of Teutonic learning which illustrate the great Nature-Myth Discovery of the nineteenth century. This particular suggestion is cited with respect and without a smile by British and American scholars. The theory concerns the birth of Dionysus. As is well known, Semele, the mother of Dionysus, being with child by Zeus, desired to see the god, but was unable to bear the divine presence, and so died; or, as others assert, she was killed by a thunderbolt launched by Hera. The child, being thus prematurely born, was taken by Zeus and carried about in his own thigh, held in by gold pins. He was afterwards secreted in Asia Minor at Mount Tmolus near Sardis. The following is a foot-note in Mr. Beckwith's edition:

"Nysa, to whose nymphs the infant Dionysos was sent, is located by Homer in Thrace.  But in later times mention is made of a Nysa in Thessaly, Eubœa, Bœotia, . . . Arabia, India, and other places."  In this uncertainty as to location, Werklein finds an indication of the origin of the Dionysiac myth, which he explains as follows: "Nysa, like Aia, the land of the golden fleece, was originally thought of as in the heavens, and was afterwards transferred to earth.  The rain-cloud, big with tempest, is the mother of Dionysos; the cloud-gathering god of the storms is his father.  When, after a flash and heavy peal of thunder, the cloud bursts in a short and, as it were, premature shower, a simple imagination conceived of this as an untimely birth of the rain from the cloud.  This naïve representation led to the personification of the cloud as Semele and the rain as Dionysos."

We may observe in this note the heavy German psychologist placing his ponderous, elephantine hypothesis carefully upon the incalculable sallies of Greek fancy; and let us observe next, the solemnity of the Anglican "Amen."  Mr. Cruickshank finds that "the analogy is, at any rate, obvious and striking."

# EURIPIDES AND GREEK GENIUS

So far as the thought goes, one can imagine Plato's introducing this very explanation of the premature birth of Dionysus into one of his dialogues. But Plato would have used it as the closing snapper of a scene, when the company were fatigued, or the subject was about to change. He would have allowed Socrates to suggest the idea demurely, just before some interruption, so as to raise a laugh and, at the same time, to escape responsibility. Socrates would, no doubt, protest that he had the story from a third party, and merely desired to know whether the company thought it important. The whole matter would thus have been left in the realm of imaginative humour, where it belongs. But the German has laid down the law of the myth as if it were a sausage; and the Englishman has swallowed the sausage and pronounced it good. Such were the Greeks; and such are the moderns.

Let us now examine the text of the *Bacchantes,* not learnedly, but casually. According to the legend, the *Bacchantes* who tore Pentheus to pieces were the followers of Dionysus, and were punishing Pentheus for his refusal to worship the new god. Pentheus and Dionysus were first-cousins, being grandsons of Cadmus by his two daughters, Agave and Semele. Cadmus was, of course, among the most respectable patriarchs of Greece, one of the Argonauts; and, at the time the story begins, he had resigned the government of Thebes, turning it over to his grandson Pentheus.

At the opening of the play Dionysus enters as Prologue, and explains that he has come disguised as a mortal with the *Bacchantes* in his train to establish his religion in Greece. He has been all over Asia Minor and now comes to Thebes, the home of his family and the first Greek city that he has entered. The smoking ruins of the palace where Hera's thunderbolt had fallen and killed his mother have now been fenced off as a sanctuary, and they form part of the palace before which the action proceeds. The god has come back to his birthplace in order to punish his mother's two sisters, who have never taken the story of his divine birth seriously, but have ridiculed his pretensions from the beginning. He has come disguised as a handsome, effeminate-looking youth, in order to move among the people and excite them before his origin is suspected. It appears that, as a result of his charms, all the women-folk of Thebes are already wandering in the mountains in Bac-

chic frenzy. Pentheus is fighting against
the new religion; but both Pentheus and
Thebes shall soon discover that Dionysus is
a god.

He closes his address to the Chorus:
"Take your drums, your native instruments
of Phrygia, the invention of Mother Rhea
and myself, and coming, beat them about
this royal palace of Pentheus, that the city
of Cadmus may see it. In the meantime I
will to the mountains, to join the rout of
bacchanal women."

The whole play is thus in full swing in a
moment; and as Dionysus makes his exit
the Mænads begin their dance. The long
opening chorus in which the wild women
chant the praises of Dionysus, has in it such
a rhythm as to bring the dancers with their
streaming hair, their fawn-skins, their great
tambourines, their Phrygian flutes and their
thyrsus-spears before the reader. Nothing
is left of all the din and frenzy, nothing of
the dancing and shouting of those inspired
Bacchantes, except the beat of their pulses
which has somehow been left in the blood of
the verse. It is impossible to read the lines,
no matter how ignorant one may be as to
the theory of Greek metres, without hearing
the thud of feet and seeing files of mad-

dened women with their heads thrown back, dancing in time, and uttering irregular, savage ejaculations that mingle with the pipes and tambourines, while the steady undertone of the words and the incessant onward drive of the circling phalanxes fling spells upon the air. The very length of this scene engulfs the reader; and, in the acting, where repetitions were no doubt resorted to, the whole amphitheatre must have been thrown into a daze and cradled to blind happiness by the brilliant, barbaric costumes, by the movement and by the music.

As the opening feature of an opera this chorus is a masterly and thrilling work. Before the dance is half finished the spectator has forgotten everything in the world except the play before him. Against this background Euripides now introduces two very old men, who are among the most sacred figures in Greek mythology,—Tiresias, the mythical soothsayer, a name as old as Homer, and Cadmus, the ancestral hero and founder,—Cadmus, the great mythic Hellene. One might almost say that these old men represent Moses and Aaron. They come in dressed for Bacchic rites, with thyrsi in their hands, garlands of ivy on their heads, —beribboned for the fray. It appears that they are converts to the new religion. They exhibit the characters of gay old *bourgeois,* delighted at their own temerity, knowing they will be laughed at, yet resolved to enjoy themselves. They are off for the mountains. The audience must have gripped its umbrellas with joy: "This is too good to be true! Is it humourous? Is it serious?" One hardly knows. But it is certainly the *best thing* ever done on the stage! The old darlings enter, meeting as by appointment, clap each other on the shoulder, admire each other's dresses, swear they will dance like good ones,—they alone of the city. "But they alone are wise! They will not be ashamed of their old age, not they! The god never intended to distinguish between old and young, but demands worship from all! They join hands in rapture (Tiresias being blind) and are about to leave, when enter the gloomy and boorish Pentheus. As a foil to the old gentlemen Pentheus is perfect. He is young, and he is angry. He now describes how all the women in his kingdom, including his mother and his two aunts, have been led off to the woods by an odious, effeminate, scented youth with long locks. The men have joined the women. It is a saturnalia of drink and debauchery. Pen-

theus has already arrested some of the women, and intends to catch the stranger and
put him in chains. One sees that Pentheus
wears already the rigidity of madness in his
eye. Although he is undoubtedly in the
right, and is the only person on the stage
with whom any sensible man can sympathise,
he is made so unpleasant, and the old men
are made so charming, that our hearts go
against decency and order.

When he reproaches Tiresias for joining
the rabble and disgracing his white hair and
his profession, Pentheus becomes so unjust
and so rude that we are against him for
being a lout. Tiresias, in a long, doddering
reply to Pentheus, now praises the divinity
of Bacchic worship, including the value of
drunkenness, speaks lightly of women's
chastity, expounds legends, describes scenery, and remains perfectly charming. Old
Cadmus adds a hint that as Dionysus is one
of the family, Pentheus ought to *pretend* to
believe in him, anyway. This is one of those
human touches that Euripides manages to
throw into the tragic scenery in some of his
plays as no one else has ever done or could
do. He surprises you with a smile in the
midst of the whirlwind. In like manner, in
the *Orestes,* when Helen cuts off a lock of

hair to lay upon the tomb of her aunt Clytemnestra, some one cries out, "See now how the hussy has cut it off in such a manner that it will not spoil her beauty. She is the same woman she always was!"

This scene of the two old men belongs among the greatest things in drama. It is beautiful; it is ridiculous; it is pathetic; it is true to nature; it is very nearly but not quite burlesque; it is in contrast to the rest of the play. The old gentlemen are a little senile, perhaps, but they are sweet-tempered, and represent all that is benign and tolerant in old age. They now join hands again, supporting each other as they leave the stage and declaring that they will pray for Pentheus and so strive to avert the punishments for his impiety. The Chorus after this departure celebrates the *vita gioiosa* in a hymn to Bacchus and Venus, and in a way so far beyond modern comprehension in its beauty and abandonment, that we are tempted to call it religious. But it is not religious. Make it a little grosser and it will be a drinking-song. But it is not a drinking-song. It is not gross: it is as refined as Praxiteles,— and as conventional. It is, in fact, a mere necessary, æsthetic member of the dramatic whole.

## GREEK GENIUS

We are taught throughout this play that anyone who resists Dionysus is an innovator, and thus all the tag-rags of prejudice against new ideas are marshalled in the choruses against Pentheus. The following is a sample: "True wisdom is to keep the heart and soul aloof from over-subtle wits. That which the less enlightened crowd approves and practises will I accept." There must be a dozen such saws scattered through the choruses, and the dramatic purpose of them is evidently to explain and justify the doom of Pentheus. Now inasmuch as Dionysus was a new god introducing a new religion, without a tradition to support him, all this appeal to tradition is ridiculous. But the alchemy of good stage-writing takes no account of logic, except stage logic. The stage is like politics. Any reasoning that will patch the plot serves the purpose. And it is absolutely necessary that the person who is going to be punished by fate in a Greek tragedy should appear to be kicking against established religious feeling. Otherwise the old stock phrases and proverbial moralities in the choruses could not be used with effect. The Mænads had no counterpart in the real life of Athens and Thebes, and we may suppose that the Athenian au-

dience accepted all these matters imagina-
tively, and as a part of the *donnée* of the
play. We do the same in accepting our stage
villains and the heroes of our fiction.

The dramatic interest in the *Bacchantes,*
from the moment when Pentheus and
Dionysus first meet, consists in watching
Dionysus "play" Pentheus (and later play
Pentheus' mother, Agave) as a fisherman
plays a trout. From one point of view it is
the most complex and finished piece of
cruelty in the world. From the dramatic
point of view it is an intense, careful, logical,
breathlessly interesting study of madness,—
that sort of madness which the Greek drama
loved, which was cast upon a man by the
gods. From the point of view of those who
garrison the modern strongholds of Learning the play is, as we have seen, a mystical
drama typifying the quiet life.

To return to the story. As soon as the
first Chorus of Mænads has finished its
strain in praise of the *vita gioiosa* there follows a picturesque scene. Dionysus is
brought in guarded, and has a verbal bout
with the tyrant Pentheus. Goethe saw an
analogy between this scene and the tableau
of Christ before Pilate; and in truth, the
situation, it must be confessed, is tremen-

dous; but the interview is conducted on a
low plane. The god is in a casuistical
mood. There is much back-talk, and *double
entendre,* and an atmosphere of drawing-
room dialectics.

"I will cast thy body into prison!"

"The god will release me."

"The god? Where is he?"

"Near me; but thine impious eyes see him
not."

"Servants, seize this fellow! He insults
me."

"You know not why you live or what you
do."

"Away with him to prison!"

If Euripides has avoided the sublime in
his handling of this judgment scene, it must
be noted that he could not have put on the
tall cothurnus of Æschylus here without re-
modelling his entire play. His Dionysus
stands throughout the drama on a level with
Pentheus, who is dealt with as an antagonist.
The scene is vital, if not noble: it is first-
rate popular drama.

The stranger god is now led off to be in-
carcerated. The Chorus sings a wild, terrible strain, calling upon Dionysus to save
himself. It is not long before the power of
the deity, who is in chains within the palace,

begins to make itself manifest. The palace
rocks, flames burst forth, and Dionysus re-
appears on the steps of the building. There
ensues an antiphonal duet between the god
and the Chorus, *fortissimo tutti*. It is tremendous: it is wonderful! The verses of
the libretto are short, but of a perfectly
amazing force. They seem to be running to
a fire. It must be that, as in modern times,
the effect of this scene was ensured by repetitions of the musical scheme; for the text of
the duet as it stands is too short to have any
carrying power.

When quiet has been restored, Dionysus
proceeds to give the Chorus a vivid account
of what happened in the stable, and of how
he frustrated the infuriated Pentheus. The
low moral tone of Dionysus' dealings with
Pentheus is maintained in this lyrical account of how he tricked and exasperated his
victim. For Pentheus, thinking to bind the
god, enchained a bull, which he found in the
stable. Breathing out fury and sweating
from his body, the madman dashed about in
the stable, while the god sat by and mocked
him. Such mockery, by the way, was, in
the Greek imagination, the worst thing that
could befall a man. There is hardly a page
of Greek tragedy which does not reveal the

fear of being laughed at, which walks like a
spectre in the Greek soul. Even Medea,
whose practical sorrows and desperate situation seem to require no such remote metaphysical motive, kills her children largely
out of fear that she will be ridiculed for her
insuccess in life.

The recitation by Dionysus of his triumph
in the stable is a sample of sustained declamation in trochaic tetrameters. Such passages seem to have been a feature in Greek
drama; and one cannot read them without
being convinced that they were accompanied
by some sort of conventional gesture. The
actor perhaps moved forward and back,
keeping time in words, gesture, and step—
probably facing the Chorus and doing a sort
of *pas seul*. Almost exactly the same kind
of business was practised on the old Italian
stage, and it survives in Rossini's operas.

The trochaic tetrameter, which in our
minds is connected with slow solemnity,
because of its use in Longfellow's "Tell me
not in mournful numbers," seems to have
been used by the Greeks in passages of
cumulative excitement, as, for instance, in
dialogues of *discovery,* where the rising
emotions of the speakers are reflected in the
jerky, shrill movement of the verse. This

metre has often been used with the same
effect in English, as, for instance, in that
dramatic lyric, "Just in time for Lanigan's
Ball." Euripides employs it here in describing the scene in the stable, where Pentheus
was dashing about with a drawn sword to
slay the god.

Pentheus now rushes on the stage, pretty
well exhausted. "I have suffered terrible
things," he shouts; "the stranger has escaped
me!" Dionysus greets him calmly. "Did I
not say or did you not hear that someone
would deliver me?" "I order ye to close
every tower all round!" shouts Pentheus to
the servants. But the god, who has now
become gentle, if not kind, promises not to
escape while they both listen to the tale of
the First Messenger.

Enter the First Messenger with those descriptions of the miraculous doings of the
Bacchantes in the forest, upon which rest
most of our modern notions about these
mysteries. The man has actually seen the
daughters of Cadmus leading the whole
Bacchic rout. At first he saw them all asleep.
Then they waked. And then "they let loose
their hair over their shoulders; and arranged
their deer-skins, as many as had had the
fastenings of their knots unloosed, and they

girded the dappled hides with serpents lick-
ing their jaws; and some having in their
arms a kid, or the wild whelps of wolves,
gave them white milk, all those who, having
lately had children, had breasts still full,
having left their infants. And they put on
their ivy chaplets, and garlands of oak and
blossoming yew. And one having taken a
thyrsus, struck it against a rock, whence a
dewy stream of water springs out; another
placed her wand on the ground, and then
the god sent up a spring of wine. . . ."

This picture of the Mænads at play is followed by another of a different sort. The
messenger, with the aid of certain shepherds,
had attacked the Bacchantes and had been
badly defeated. "We then, flying, avoided
the tearing of the Bacchæ, but they sprang
on the heifers browsing the grass with un-
armed hand, and you might see one rending
asunder a fatted lowing calf, and others rent
open cows, and you might see either ribs, or
a cloven-footed hoof, tossed here and there.
And hanging beneath the pine-trees the fragments were dripping, dabbled in gore; and
the fierce bulls, before showing their fury
with their horns, were thrown to the ground,
overpowered by myriads of maidens' hands.
For their pointed spear was not made

bloody, but the women, hurling the thyrsi from their hands, wounded them, and turned their backs to flight, women defeating men; not without the aid of some god. And they went back again to the place whence they had departed, to the same fountains which the god had caused to spring up for them, and they washed off the blood; and the snakes with their tongues cleansed the drops from their cheeks. . . ."

The effect of this tale is to harden Pentheus the more. He orders out the troops. Nothing can dissuade him. The messenger warns; Dionysus begs him to submit. Dionysus even offers to go himself to the mountains and fetch the revellers to Thebes. But Pentheus suspects a trick of some sort, and clamours for his arms. It is at this point, and while Pentheus is plainly blear-eyed with enchantment, that Dionysus suggests a clever ruse,—namely, that Pentheus and he shall visit the mountains together and ensconce themselves in some safe hiding-place from which to view the sport. Pentheus shall go disguised as a woman, and the god will dress him and guide him to the spot. They will pass through the city together, following deserted byways; they will spy upon the mysteries. Pentheus' eyes gleam

with excitement, and he goes off the stage
to assume the required dress. Dionysus follows him, waiting only to throw to the
Chorus a lyric vaunt, "O Women, the man
is in the toils, and he will come to the Bacchæ, where, dying, he will pay the penalty."

The time during which the change of
clothes is accomplished is occupied by the
Chorus in a pæan of exultant triumph over
the impious man; and then re-enter Dionysus leading Pentheus dressed as a woman.
The unfortunate wretch is in the clutches of
mania. He sees two suns, and Thebes appears to him as if twinned into two cities.

"How do I look? Do I look like my
mother, or like my aunt Ino?"

"Very like them; but this lock of hair is
out of place."

"I disarranged it in practising the Bacchic
steps."

"Let me set it right. But hold up your
head! And your girdle is crooked, and your
fringes hang awry."

"My right leg is all wrong, I admit; but
the robe on the other side seems about correct. Should I hold the thyrsus in my right
hand or in the left?"

"Now you are perfect."

"I feel as if I could bear the whole moun-

tain on my shoulders, Bacchantes and all. I
lay my hand to terrible things."

"You are terrible; and terrible are the
sufferings that are to follow. Your renown
shall reach to heaven."

It is impossible to suggest in English the
woven tissue of sarcasm of the Greek text
throughout the play. The brilliancy of shot
meanings, one sparkling from behind the
other, was a passion with the Greeks. They
loved it as they loved encrusted gold.

Here, in this scene of the dressing up of
Pentheus, we have comic writing of gigantic
effectiveness; for it is both comic and tragic.
The malignant deity attacks his victim with
gibes of irony. It will be remembered that
in the scene between Faust and Mephistopheles where the helplessness of mortals
in the presence of supernatural power is
the point in demonstration, Goethe makes
Mephistopheles put Faust to sleep, and then
laugh in an aside, "Du bist noch nicht der
Mann den Teufel fest zu halten!" So mild
are the moderns; so terrible were the an-
cients.

What makes us shudder is not so much
the idea of a god manipulating a mortal, as
the manner in which it is carried out. No
modern could bear either to write or to wit-

ness the cruelties practised by Dionysus
upon Pentheus. In those places where the
god deals gently, it is with a cat-and-mouse
malevolence; and in the later scenes of the
play Dionysus' *asides* have, as Mr. Cruickshank remarks, the ferocity of a wild beast.
We ought to judge of these horrors not
rashly, but by the light of that whole system
of conventional horror, and the stage symbols of horror, which were developed by the
Greek theatre and which will be discussed
later herein.

While we pause to take an ice in the foyer
between the acts of this terrific drama, let us
recall the words of the good Mr. Tyrrell,
who finds "an ethical contentment and speculative calm" in the play.

After the joint departure of Pentheus and
Dionysus for the mountains, the Chorus
sing another pæan—"Go, ye fleet hounds of
madness, go to the mountains where the
daughters of Cadmus hold their company;
drive them raving against the fanatic man
who came to spy on the Mænads,—him in
woman's attire," etc. We have not long to
wait for news of the expedition; for the
Second Messenger arrives almost immediately and gives a blood-curdling description of how the miserable Pentheus has been

murdered by his own mother, Agave. We begin to feel that the climax is approaching, and we are not disappointed; for, before we can draw breath, Agave enters, carrying in her arms the gory head of her son, which she believes to be the head of a mountain lion. We now realise that Agave's conversion has been the work of a madness superinduced by the god in punishment for her former apostasy. She is still out of her wits, and boasts of killing the lion with her own hands. She pets the head, comments on its crest, fondles its soft hair. She is interrogated by the Chorus; she is urged gently forward from point to point till every shade of her delirious vanity touching her imaginary prowess as a huntress is exposed, and every depth of humiliation is gently touched.

In this scene we have the substance and climax of Greek tragedy,—namely, horror. The manner, also, in which the whole has moved forward, its sheets of coruscating irony, its flashes of godlike power exercised against the worm, show the triumph and climax of Greek method.

The destruction of Pentheus and of Agave is followed by a scene very characteristic of Euripides,—namely, a scene of

secondary pathos, the drip under the eaves
after the storm has passed. Cadmus and
his wife are dismissed by the sorrowing
Dionysus, and are compelled to wander
away to other lands, being drawn in an ox-
cart. This outcome is a part of the legend,
and is therefore excellent play-writing.
From the point of view of justice the outcome is absurd; for the pious Cadmus had
welcomed the god. But for stage purposes
a "condoling" scene was needed. After the
rending and the madness one must have a
little quiet weeping to accompany the sad
return to one's senses; it ends the play better. Just so, in the *Hippolytus*, the gory,
dying son of Theseus is brought back upon
the stage for a scene of reconciliation with
his now penitent father. Euripides the
Human, with his droppings of warm tears,
comes round with his mop at the end of the
play, and the nice old *contadina* is waiting
to receive her pittance—which we had forgotten—as we leave the box.

The complex finale of the *Bacchantes* is
arrived at slowly, and many beauties lie scattered along the way, some of them obvious,
like the sudden appearance of Dionysus and
the shattering of the palace walls; many of
them incommunicable, like the changes in

the verse-forms and the swing of many
pounding, sing-song metres, which would be
intolerable in English, yet are beautiful in
Greek. Such is the *Bacchantes* of Euripides. You cannot touch it anywhere
without receiving a shock. There is not a
moment in the course of the play which does
not tingle.

# V

THE *Bacchantes,* like every other Greek
play, is the result, first, of the legend;
second, of the theatre. There is always
some cutting and hacking, due to the difficulty of getting the legend into the building.
Legends differ as to their dramatic possi-
bilities, and the incidents which are to be put
on the stage must be selected by the poet.
The site of the play must be fixed. Above
all, a Chorus must be arranged for.

The choosing of a Chorus is indeed one
of the main problems of the tragedian. If
he can hit on a natural sort of Chorus he is
a made man. In the *Alcestis* we saw that
the whole background of grief and wailing
was one source of the charm of the play.
Not only are the tragic parts deepened, but
the gayer scenes are set off by this feature.
If the fable provides no natural and obvious
Chorus, the playwright must bring his
Chorus on the stage by stretching the

imagination of the audience. He employs a group of servants or of friends of the hero; if the play is a marine piece, he uses sailors. The whole atmosphere of his play depends upon the happiness of his choice.

In the *Agamemnon* "the old men left at home" form the Chorus. There is enough dramatic power in this one idea to carry a play. It is so natural: the old men are on the spot; they are interested; they are the essence of the story, and yet external to it. These old men are, indeed, the archetype of all choruses,—a collection of bystanders, a sort of little dummy audience, intended to steer the great, real audience into a comprehension of the play.

The Greek dramatist found this very useful machine, the Chorus, at his elbow; but he was, on the other hand, greatly controlled by it. It had ways of its own: it inherited dramatic necessities. The element of convention is so very predominant in the handling of Greek choruses by the poets, that we have in chorus work something that may be regarded almost as a constant quality. By studying choruses one can arrive at an idea of the craft of Greek play-writing,—one can even separate the conventional from the personal, to some extent.

# EURIPIDES AND GREEK GENIUS

The Greek Chorus has no mind of its own; it merely gives echo to the last dramatic thought. It goes forward and back, contradicts itself, sympathises with all parties or none, and lives in a limbo. Its real function is to represent the slow-minded man in the audience. It does what he does, it interjects questions and doubts, it delays the plot and indulges in the proper emotions during the pauses. These functions are quite limited, and were completely understood in Greek times; so much so, that in the typical stock tragedy of the Æschylean school certain saws, maxims, and reflections appear over and over again. One of them, of course, was, "See how the will of the gods works out in unexpected ways." Another, "Let us be pious, and reverence something that is perhaps behind the gods themselves." Another, "This is all very extraordinary: let us hope for the best." Another, "Our feelings about right and wrong must somehow be divine; traditional morality, traditional piety, are somehow right."

Precisely the same reflections are often put in the mouths of the subordinate characters, and for precisely the same purpose. "O may the quiet life be mine! Give me neither poverty nor riches: for the destinies of the great are ever uncertain." "Temptation leads to insolence, and insolence to destruction"; and so forth. Such reflections serve the same purpose, by whomever they are uttered. They underscore the moral of the story and assure the spectator that he has not missed the point.

As religious tragedy broadened into political and romantic tragedy, the Chorus gained a certain freedom in what might be called its interjectional duty,—its duty, that is to say, of helping the plot along by proper questions. It gained also a Protean freedom in its emotional interpretations during pauses. The playwrights apparently discovered that by the use of music and dancing, the most subtle and delicate—nay, the most whimsical—varieties of lyrical mood could be conveyed to great audiences. In spite of this license, however, the old duties of the Chorus as guardians of conservative morality remained unchanged; and the stock phrases of exhortation and warning remained *de rigueur* in the expectation of the audience. Their meaning had become so well known that by the time of Æschylus they were expressed in algebraic terms.

No man could to-day unravel a Chorus of Æschylus if only one such Chorus existed.

EURIPIDES AND GREEK GENIUS

The truncated phrases and elliptical
thoughts are clear to us because we have
learned their meaning through reiteration,
and because they always mean the same
thing. The poet has a license to provide the
Chorus with dark sayings,—dark in form,
but simple in import. It was, indeed, his
duty to give these phrases an oracular character. In the course of time such phrases
became the terror of the copyists. Obscure
passages became corrupt in process of transcription; and thus we have inherited a whole
class of choral wisdom which we understand *well enough* (just as the top gallery
understood it *well enough*) to help us in our
enjoyment of the play. The obscurity, and
perhaps even some part of what we call
"corruption," are here a part of the stage
convention.

Now with regard to the *Bacchantes,* the
scheme of having Mænads for a Chorus
gave splendid promise of scenic effect; and
the fact that, as a logical consequence, these
ladies would have to give utterance to the
usual maxims of piety, mixed in with the
rhapsodies of their professional madness,
did not daunt Euripides. He simply makes
the Chorus do the usual chorus work without burdening his mind about character-

drawing. Thus the Mænads, at moments when they are not pretending to be Mænads, and are not singing, "Away to the mountains, O the foot of the stag," and so on, are obliged to turn the other cheek and pretend to be interested bystanders, old gaffers wagging their beards and quoting the book of Proverbs. The transition from one mood to the other is done in a stroke of lightning, and seems to be independent of the music. That is, it *seems* to make no difference, so long as the musical schemes are filled out, whether the ladies are singing, "On with the dance, let joy be unconfined!" or, "True wisdom differs from sophistry, and consists in avoiding subjects that are beyond mortal comprehension." All such discrepancies would, no doubt, have been explained if we possessed the music; but the music is lost. It seems, at any rate, certain that the grand public was not expected to understand the word-for-word meaning of choruses; hence their license to be obscure. We get the same impression from the gibes of Aristophanes, whose ridicule of the pompous obscurity of Æschylus makes us suspect that the audiences could not follow the grammar in the lofty parts of tragedy. They accepted the drum-roll of horror, and understood the

larger grammar of tragedy, much as we are
now forced to do in reading the plays.

It would seem that by following the technique of tragedy, and by giving no thought
to small absurdities, Euripides got a double effect out of his Mænads, and no one
observed that anything was wrong. In one
place he resorts to a dramatic device, which
was perhaps well known in his day,—
namely, the "conversion" of a bystander.
After the First Messenger has given the
great description of Dionysus' doings in the
mountains, the Chorus, or one of them, with
overpowering yet controlled emotion, steps
forward and says, "I tremble to speak free
words in the presence of my king; yet nevertheless be it said: Dionysus is no less a
god than the greatest of them!" This reference to the duty of a subject is probably
copied from a case where the Chorus was
made up of local bystanders. In the mouth
of a Mænad the proclamation is logically
ridiculous; yet so strange are the laws of
what "goes" on the stage that it may have
been effective even here.

Some of the choruses in the *Bacchantes*
are miracles of poetic beauty, of savage passion, of liquid power. It is hard to say
exactly what they are, but they are wonder-

ful. And behind all there gleams from the
whole play a sophistication as deep as the
Ægean. We observe it in little things, in
points scored during the thrust and parry
of argument, in the drawing-room tone of
the whole discussion, and in a feeling as of a
*compte rendu—quod erat demonstrandum*
—at the end, where Dionysus lowers his
rapier and bows to the public like a toreador.

*Aga.* O Dionysus! we have sinned; thy
    pardon we implore.
*Dio.* Too late have ye learned to know me;
    ye knew me not at the proper time.
*Aga.* We recognise our error; but thou art
    too revengeful.
*Dio.* Yea, for I, though a god, was slighted
    by you.
*Aga.* Gods should not let their passions
    sink to man's level.
*Dio.* Long ago my father Zeus ordained it
    thus.
*Aga.* Alas! my aged sire, our doom is
    fixed; 'tis woeful exile.
*Dio.* Why then delay the inevitable?

Euripides has put the legend into the
frame very simply. He merely assumes that
Dionysus is in the right. Dionysus was

justly offended: it was impiety not to recognise him. The proof of this is in the outcome.
It is the old *motif:* defiance of deity punished by madness.  But in the treatment the
horrors are worked up so vengefully, and
the god becomes so vindictive, that there is
danger lest the whole thing may appear to
be a travesty on religion.  Even in Greek
times the character of a god was supposed to
bear some relation to natural goodness.  It
would not do to make him out too unjust.

  The *Bacchantes* strains one's sense of justice, but arouses admiration for the way in
which Euripides has worked the time-hon-
oured machinery of the drama to new
effects.  By one more turn of the screw he
has got a new situation,—yet an old one.
Perhaps people may think he is using this
machinery irreverently, and intends to
throw a light backward upon the whole
structure of Olympus.  If ever there was a
play calculated to confuse the sense of right
and wrong, it is the *Bacchantes.*  Yet it is
all legitimate.  He has not transgressed: his
mouth is full of piety; he is a conservative.
Some people even regard the *Bacchantes* as
Euripides' recantation, a sort of apology for
earlier free-thinking, a profession of faith.
The trouble with this theory is that the mat-

ter is a little overdone: the cure is worse
than the disease. One suspects that a caus-
tic wit may somewhere lurk concealed
beneath the new pietism of the old-time
sceptic. Is he laughing at his enemies, and
will they find it out and punish him in the
end? Such thoughts hover in the mind of
the reader of the *Bacchantes,* and may have
arisen in the mind of him that wrote it.
Euripides may have distrusted the play. At
any rate, the fact remains that he did not
publish it in his lifetime.

Heresy in Greek times seems to have become identified with "reason." There was
no dogma in the Greek religion, so that when
clever and sceptical persons began to think
and to talk, nothing very definite could be
urged against them, except that they were
too clever by half, and had better shut up or
they would get into trouble. This situation
made life at Athens more uncertain than if
there had existed a well-organised inquisi-
tion. Heresy trials have always been a kind
of epidemic. In one year they are in the air
and infect politics; in another, not. If there
be no dogma and no religious tribunals, the
free-thinker is at the mercy of the mob.
The French Revolution shows the practical
dangers which arise when the vague "sound-

ness" of a man's opinions begins to be questioned by a popular assembly. The execution of Socrates occurred five years after Euripides' death.

The expressions of conservatism in the *Bacchantes* are tightened to an unendurable rigidity. They do not solace, but torment. This is part of the slight overscrewing which is apparent in other members of the play. The older Greek dramas had depicted a hero while he was being maddened by the gods,—the gods, of course, remaining unseen. Euripides brings the god on the stage and uses the *maddener,* not the maddened, as his protagonist. In doing so he gives a brilliant picture of a demon, calls him a god, and then stands, like Torquemada, proclaiming the sanctity of the faith: he is ready to die for it. All this makes a very remarkable play, and one which has puzzled the elect. The play is undoubtedly a great *jeu d'esprit,* —one of the greatest,—but it is a *jeu d'esprit* only by accident; it is, primarily, merely a play. Euripides arrived at these remarkable effects by following out æsthetic laws and by developing well-established principles. The moral and theological bearings of his work may even have surprised or a little disconcerted the author himself.

[83]

## GREEK GENIUS

As a monument of the Greek Genius the *Bacchantes* is more instructive than if it belonged to the unapproachable class,—to those masterpieces of Art which defy criticism. The work is decadent. It would be an overstatement to say that the *Bacchantes* is the *reductio ad absurdum* of Greek tragedy. It is merely a great work of art, in which the *intentions* are a little more accentuated, the *nuances* a little more pronounced, than the greatest period would have permitted. It represents a decline in art, an overstimulation, a wringing of the emotions such as audiences seem to require after they have begun to weary of the calmest and greatest kinds of art. The sculpture of Praxiteles, and Greek sculpture just after Praxiteles' time, betray the same subtle overaccentuation, the same mordant charm and power to draw blood, that Euripides possessed on the stage. The artists of this epoch know their trade almost too well. There is a little virtuosity in Euripides, which certain natures have always resented, both in ancient and in modern times.

The highly specialised character of Greek drama may be seen by examining any complete play. The field of idea was small, as we know; and the mode and process of pres-

# EURIPIDES AND GREEK GENIUS

entation were categorical. Certain "features" followed each other on the stage.
There was, for instance, the prologue; there
was the word-hacking, line-for-line dialogue, the recitation by messengers, the
antiphony of soloist and Chorus, the anapæs-
tic passages, the dactylic passages, etc.
There was the ironical scene in which every
word was shadowed by a menacing secondary meaning. Each of these matters
was governed by rule, and had an interest
and a tradition of its own. The choruses
were as complex as a ritual, provided at
enormous expense by private munificence,
and criticised with learning and rigour by
the connoisseurs.

The Greek national life was in some sort
reflected in this great mirror, the theatre.
Down in the middle of the auditorium
stands the Chorus, representing the people
at large. On the stage move the myths, to
wit, Greek Education. The irradiations of
wit and cynicism, of piety and enthusiasm,
of national feeling and local politics, flash
through the amphitheatre as from a great
reflector, and we who step back into it, even
in imagination or for a moment, are
strangely played upon by natural force.
The whole Greek mind is here,—one deliver-

[85]

ance of the whole mind, one form of its
crystallisation. In the *Bacchantes* we can
see the machinery a little too plainly. The
plot is a little too evident, the members of
the drama are a little too well articulated,
the irony too continuous. The Mænads are
too interesting,—one feels that their head-
dresses have been made by an expensive mil-
liner, and copied from a tomb in Thrace.
Dionysus is a model of loveliness, but
decadent. Observe his love-lock and his
walk. The recitations of the messengers are
beautifully "mounted" by words of prepara-
tion, but mounted ever so little too high.
The text of them gives a glance at the pit
and says, "Watch me do this!" At the end
of the Second Messenger's speech, where
the reciter crouches and slinks off the stage
rather than meet Agave (whose dreadful
affliction he has been describing, and who is
to enter behind him), we feel that the actor
has scored a success. There is something
about all of it that reminds us of the art of
Louis XIV. I am saying this not so much
in order to disparage Euripides as to throw
light upon the greater work behind Euripides, and which, by reason of its perfection, we cannot criticise. These defects of
Euripides seem to give a cue to the Greek

mind. The cue is *sophistication*. The Greek temple is scarcely more conventional than the Greek play. Every part has its function. "So such things should be," says the Athenian. Any other disposition seemed to him to be ugly. What has been found to go well on the stage must be put on the stage. There were plenty of dramatic themes which he never discovered, just as there are other forms of architecture which in Greek hands might have rivalled the temple. But the Greek mind turns away from experiments. The Greek seeks for such solutions of things as are conformable to his climate, his surroundings, his civic life, his sport, his conversation and humour. He has no imagination for things outside of his world; but within the limits of his world he has thought everything out with a fineness of perception and an accuracy of statement never known before nor since.

There is one region of thought which the modern and the Greek mind have in common,—namely, the world of æsthetics and of æsthetic criticism. We cannot define this world. We only know one thing for certain about it: that it is pleasant. It is a pleasure-loving world, where philosophy is the butler that hands the tea-things. When a modern

GREEK GENIUS

man first walks into one of Plato's dialogues,
or reads a play of Sophocles, he feels like a
boor entering a palace. They are all so
clever, these Greek princes, and give the
retort courteous and the quip modest without effort. They deal with many ideas
which we think we understand, yet they
arrange them in a way that we never could
have imagined. They all seem to be playing
a celestial game of irony. They are like
Arabian merchants, who talk by gestures,
and carry on mystical transactions above the
comprehension of the intruding modern
mind. Aristophanes is the greatest of them,
because he alone has realised that the whole
business is gigantic buffoonery, and that to
laugh is the sincerest thing in the end.

This quality of irony is a thing peculiarly
and typically Greek. It was sedulously cultivated by the Greeks, and was considered to
be a concomitant of intellect. It is found
even in Homer. Irony seems to consist in
the consciousness that the thing said is not
the whole truth. The difference between
Aristophanes and other Greek humourists is
that he laughs out, while the rest merely
smile or gaze calmly on the sea. Suppressed
humour and silent mockery are things which
hardly exist in the modern Anglo-Saxon

[88]

world, where the club and truncheon are in
order rather than the stiletto and the in-
nuendo. There have always been Italian
poets, however, who possessed sardonic
humour, and French writers with subtle,
quiet irony. The whole tone of mind to
which this kind of humour is native belongs
rather to the Mediterranean than to the
north of Europe. It goes with less heart and
with more wit than the Teuton possesses.
In dealing with anything Greek one must
always be ready for an "aside." It may be
a stab, or it may be a mere gesture, which
arouses the afterthought in one's mind,—
"Ah, that's what the fellow meant, is it?"
The Greek comic statuettes have this same
quizzical humour. All these things, both
the writings and the statues, make the modern feel like a barbarian, because of their
subtlety.

Greek art, nevertheless, has always been
full of significance to the barbarians. After
some converse with these refined Hellenes
we begin to benefit by their cultivation.
Take, for instance, the Greek power of enjoyment. What other race ever made enjoyment into a religion? At first we are
shocked and unhinged by the idea, but soon
we begin to "respond." It makes us more

suave and limber to think that pleasure is a
legitimate pursuit. We soon learn to take
a share in the feast, almost a hand in the
game.

What the Greeks took up they treated
with such logical completeness as to impart
a symbolic character to the product. If you
erect a perfect sphere you erect a symbol;
and very likely other people will see in it
intimations of philosophy. If a gymnast
throws a disc with absolute grace, someone
in the amphitheatre is pretty sure to think
him a hero. This very play, the *Bacchantes,*
by reason of its organic, logical perfection,
has become a parable to many people. Who
shall limit the meanings of a Greek poet, or
decree what visions men shall have in gazing
into a crystal? Happy those who have them!

The *Bacchantes* is like an old, abandoned
farm-wagon which lies on its back in the
woods with its wheels in the air, and which
from time to time is discovered by small parties of savage boys. The boys say: "Come!
Let us pretend that this is a fire-engine. See
how the wheels turn about! Run, run!
Fire, fire!" The wheels go round, and the
boys shout with sincere joy. And yet the
machine is not a fire-engine, but a wagon;
and the *Bacchantes* is not an allegorical

fable, but a play,—the fiercest play ever written.

To return to the drama. The sophistication of the Greek mind is what stimulates the modern. The Greek could count up to one hundred in art; we only to seventy-five. We misinterpret him through crediting that to emotion which is merely due to convention. For instance, the hideous cruelty of Greek tragedy is largely conventional, plastic, contrapuntal. It was in following this inner logic that the audience found pleasure, somewhat as we find pleasure at a modern concert in following the inner logic of a very complex sonata. There are no facts in music, and so in Greek tragedy there are no facts. It is all an intellectual *schema,* or progression of ideas, built up and led on towards a climax. All the externals of the Greek Drama are intentionally and obviously unreal. They must operate only as hints to the imagination; otherwise the illusion will be destroyed. If you tack a real bow-knot upon the picture of a child, you will destroy the life of the picture. So, on the Greek stage all realism is avoided. For instance, when Agave comes upon the scene with the head of her son in her arms, she is carrying a *papier-mâché* image of a head, much above

life-size, and painted with gore. The body
of Pentheus consists of fragments which are
brought upon the stage immediately afterwards. The only proper stage handling of
such scenes as this, which were not unusual
in Greek tragedy, is the marionette system:
"Here is Charlemagne, here is the head of
the Soldan," etc. Thus alone can the story
be kept upon its true stage in the mind. If
you tell a bloody history to a child, *and keep
the setting unreal,* it makes no difference
what atrocities the plot involves. In Greece
the stage language (*i.e.,* the verse-forms,
the dresses, and the acting) was provided
by custom, and the playwright was expected
to stick at nothing in the use of them. They
are a kind of great alphabet which must be
accepted *in toto.*

There is a wide-spread belief that the
Greeks avoided the horrible. This is, perhaps, founded on Horace's remark that
Medea does not slaughter her children before the public. In any event, the belief
seems not to correspond with the facts. The
Greeks seem to adopt any dramatic device
that will arouse horror most effectually.
Now it is infinitely more effective to have
Medea's children slain by their mother's
hand just behind the scenes, where their

unavailing cries can be heard by the audience, than to have her kill them before the footlights. So, also, in the slaughter of Agamemnon, the prolonged deliberation of the Chorus—who confer as to whether or not it is their duty to do anything about the murder, vying with one another in the senselessness and incompetence of their suggestions, while the howls of Agamemnon fill the theatre—is more horrible than any murder on the stage could possibly have been made. So, too, in Euripides' *Orestes,* after Orestes and Pylades have entered the palace for the purpose of murdering Helen, there is an awe-striking moment when the Chorus hears someone coming down the path, and fears lest the whole dreadful plot may fail. The cries of Helen have been heard, but are not decisive. Neither the Chorus nor the audience knows just what is happening, and this uncertainty intensifies the horror. There are moments in *Macbeth* where the same situation is staged by almost the same methods. These breathless pauses in tragedy are due to the fact that the unseen is more dreadful than the seen.

But there is an independent reason for the avoidance of death itself on the Greek stage. If personages were not permitted to die

there, it is because there was no way of getting rid of the bodies. The slain could not
get up and walk off, or be carried off, without introducing a ridiculous element. Alcestis is allowed to die on the stage because the
circumstances make it possible to remove
her body dramatically.

How ineffectual in appearance are kill-
ings in real life! A man is shot, or struck
by a train, or jumps from a burning building. It is all over in a moment; it is *terne,*
it is voiceless, it is real. The Greek stage
avoids horrors of this kind because they are
not dramatically useful; but the Greek stage
has horrors of its own that are worse than
they.

The Elizabethan drama, which had no
special laws or conventions, but tried everything, used sometimes to indulge in realistic
horrors. Such things, however, proved to
be disgusting rather than horrible. They
reveal in their authors an imperfect acquaintance with dramatic law. If you set
upon the stage Thyestes eating a pie made
of his own children's flesh, and if you make
him fall backward in convulsions when he
learns of what he has done, you can never
make the scene as awful as it becomes
through the horror of a third party who

gives an account of it. The emotion must be instrumental. All the inner resonance of the drama will be interrupted by any appeal that comes from realism. Everything that happens on the stage must be taken up into the whirling symphony of the whole performance, the value and force of each element being assigned to it by the poet.

# VI

## PROFESSOR GILBERT MURRAY—OXFORD

PROFESSOR GILBERT MURRAY is the best known scholar in the British Empire, and is the most widely beloved scholar of the present epoch. Whatever be his claims to learning as weighed in the Plutonic haunts of technical work (of which the nether gods alone are cognisant), his enormous literacy and his easy command over the whole book-world appear like a miracle to the general reader. Beneath the authority of his official post and the necromancy of his erudition walks a literary talent of a very high order. His suavity, his personal charm, his real humility, his humour, his freedom from dogmatism, the Orpheus-like serenity with which he walks through the Plutonic regions, illuminating scholarship as he goes with the interest of a fairy-tale, make him the adored friend of every reader. *The Rise of the Greek Epic* seems to be the book which modern educa-

tion was waiting for, the book that should
recover to literature the lost territory which
the whirlpools of archæology and etymology
had eaten away, and should reinstate Humanism as the Regent of Learning.

This book, *The Rise of the Greek Epic,* is
a review of modern speculation as to the
form of Homer's poems. Its main thesis
is simple, and its methods are the critical and
verifiable methods of modern research. Yet
no one can read the book without having his
conceptions enlarged, not only as touching
Greek literature, but as touching the whole
history of literary expression.

The province of criticism is, however, but
one field of Professor Murray's activity.
There are two Murrays, and they bear a
somewhat paradoxical relation to each
other. There is Murray the critical scholar,
whose work has an imaginative, stimulating
value to the student of Greek; and there is
Murray the author of poetic translations,
chiefly of Euripides, whose work is essentially non-critical, even anti-critical, and
who fulfils to the student of Greek literature
the office of an *ignis fatuus.*

If in the following paper a protest is
made against the last mentioned side of
Murray's influence, this is because of the

EURIPIDES AND GREEK GENIUS

magnitude of his influence, and because of
the subtlety of the questions involved, which
make sharp speaking necessary to clearness.
Murray the critic is the genial scholar
named above. In *The Rise of the Greek
Epic* he enters the field of Homeric criticism. Now the Homeric Question during
the last one hundred and fifty years became
a great bazaar: it is like a covered market a
hundred yards long,—a *halle,*—filled with
furiously active tailors and sewers of patchwork. They sit upon piles of bagging, each
in his booth heaped with bales of work.
Slaves stagger to and fro under new and
miscellaneous plunder which the archæologists are momently consigning to the bazaar
from the quarried ruins of every Mediterranean shore. Bearded men wrangle, and
dim-eyed enthusiasts attack their theses.
They rip and sew, sift and assay, they heap
and scatter like madmen. The general
reader looks upon the scene in smiles and in
despair. Then Murray enters and begins
talking in a casual way about Homer. He
is very gentle. Anyone can understand
what he says. He is explaining what some
of the fury is about. He comes from the
open air and brings the daylight with him.
He is as likely to illustrate a point with

something that he saw in the street five minutes before as with a line from the Pen-
tateuch. He is going to show you what sort
of a thing literature was in its beginnings.
He pauses over a pile of manuscripts as he
enters, picks up one, and shows its drift. A
slave passes with an armful of broken crock-
ery. He begs pardon of the slave, borrows
a potsherd for a moment, and illustrates his
idea with it; returns it, and passes on. We
follow him through the emporium, and in
an hour or two we come to understand
something about the Homeric pandemo-
nium. We know not how much is Murray's
own, or to what extent he is an interpreter
of others; but before he has finished his
rounds we become convinced that his general view must be true. Something of the
sort is indubitably the true view. That the
Iliad and Odyssey are in their living merits
a part of the great Attic period in Greek
literature; that they are archaic and artificial
in their language; that, in the form in which
we know them, they represent the last recen-
sion of a body of myth which is hundreds of
years old; that no categorical answer is to
be looked for as to any of the detailed questions about their origin,—these things we
believe and see to be true after reading the

book, in the same manner as if we had discovered them for ourselves. And this is what Murray desires to make us perceive.

The secret of Murray's power seems to lie in the truth that illustration is more telling than argument. His art keeps his thesis afloat and throws the glamour of a fairy-tale upon the dreadful citations. You are ever in a magic sea strewn with argosies of Oriental plunder. Meanwhile, Gilbert Murray himself is before you, the man of the afternoon chat, as modern and familiar a figure as London can show. Here is the triumph of British cultivation. There is a good sense and a good humour about the book, a non-dogmatic social element. Here is seen the same *bonhomie* and avoidance of extremes which are at the bottom of England's political greatness.

The second Murray—namely, the versifier and translator of Euripides—must now be considered. He is an English poet of a very definite literary ancestry. He belongs to the old Neo-Hellenic Oxford teaching,—one might almost call it a school of thought. He is a scion of that traditional English scholarship of which Matthew Arnold and Swinburne are examples. This tradition is wider than a mere school of poetry: it is a caste of thought, and a mode of æsthetic, quasi-moral feeling.

Let the reader recall Mallock's *New Republic,* which remains as the best monument of a distinct historic eddy in the thought and influence of Oxford. This little swirl was not more than an eddy: it never comprehended the whole of Oxford even in its day of plenitude.

Mallock gently ridiculed the poses of this Christian-Pagan University Humanism in his famous mock-sermon, which was supposed to represent Jowett's manner. In another place he makes Jowett say: "Christianity includes all other religions, even any honest denial of itself."

In this phrase of Mallock's we have the philosophic crux of the whole matter. Gilbert Murray the poet is an aftermath of this Victorian culture, and in his mouth are the charming accents of all that old-fashioned, tinted cultivation. This cultivation is precious, mannered, Euphuistic. If accepted as part of the drawing-room, where the lights are shaded, this music is not unpleasing. There is a *sordino* on every instrument, and none but the sweetest resolutions are permitted. But when daylight meets the page and brings this school of

musing into competition with open-air literature, its weaknesses are revealed. It is all
candy. It belongs, indeed, to that class of
artificial work, not without value, of which
many epochs, including the twelfth century
and the Renaissance, have provided examples. Walter Pater's books are of the same
school. We must remember the *Cortegiano*
in reading them. There is only one point of
view from which Murray's translations can
arouse antagonism, or even just reproba-
tion,—namely, when they are used as an
introduction to Greek literature.

Gilbert Murray the poet has a note, a
charm, a lyric gift of his own. The following verses from the *Hippolytus* are an example of his genius. The whole translation
is very nearly equal to them in sweetness.
They may serve to remind the reader of this
author's merits:

"Could I take me to some cavern for mine
      hiding,
  In the hilltops where the sun scarce
      hath trod;
Or a cloud make the home of mine
      abiding,
  As a bird among the bird-droves of
      God!

[ 103 ]

# GREEK GENIUS

Could I wing me to my rest amid the
    roar
Of the deep Adriatic on the shore,
Where the waters of Eridanus are clear,
    And Phaeton's sad sisters by his grave
Weep into the river, and each tear
    Gleams, a drop of amber, in the wave:

To the strand of the daughters of the
    Sunset,
    The Apple-tree, the singing and the
        gold;
Where the mariner must stay him from
    his onset,
    And the red wave is tranquil as of old;
    Yea, beyond that Pillar of the End
    That Atlas guardeth, would I wend;
Where a voice of living waters never
    ceaseth
    In God's quiet garden by the sea,
And Earth, the ancient life-giver, in-
    creaseth
    Joy among the meadows, like a tree."

This is very charming, but not very
Greek. There is, in spite of its merits, a
monotony of feeling about this and other
Hellenising British poetry, and a certain
preoccupation with God, which are not

found in Greek. There is generally a sense of variety in Greek poetry and a substratum of wit or shrewdness. The plaintive note and the highly moral note, which the British Victorian School so much affects, do occur now and then in Greek, but they do not predominate. Of course all mythology deals with gods; and by translating every reference to Olympus with a big *G,* this school has produced some very interesting literary flavours. Religion is their pet thought. They are not satisfied unless they have stitched Greek religion (whatever it was) and English religion (whatever it ought to be) into some sort of harmony. In their works the Bible is subtly alluded to through the use of biblical words, and Dionysus and Christ are delicately jumbled.

There is, it must be confessed, a little too much gentleness everywhere in the æsthetic literature of modern England, as if a drop of sweet oil had been added to life. All this comes from a genuine, intimately English, ethical development; traces of it may be seen in Tennyson. These English gentlemen are admirable fellows, and the world is better and richer for them in many ways. But it is impossible to remain in the state of mind in which they live and to render the

Greek drama, because their vehicle is one which transmutes everything into falsetto sentiment.

The Greek genius is so different from the modern English genius that the two cannot understand each other. How shall we come to see this clearly? The matter is difficult in the extreme because we are all soaked in modern feeling, and in America we are all drenched in British influence. The desire of Britain to annex ancient Greece, the deep-felt need that the English writers and poets of the nineteenth century have shown to edge and nudge nearer to Greek feeling, is familiar to all of us. Browning expresses his Hellenic longings by paraphrasing Greek myths; Swinburne, by his hymeneal strains; Matthew Arnold, by sweetness and light; Gilbert Murray, by sweetness and pathos; and all through the divine right of Victorian expansion.

It has been a profoundly unconscious development in all of these men. They have instinctively and innocently attached their views of life to Euripides and to the other great Attic writers. In doing so they have developed a whole artificial language of their own, as conventional as the language of Homer. And, curiously enough, there is not

to be found in the whole length and breadth
of letters a dialect more unlike the Greek
than the jargoning of this especial school of
warblers. The reason is that the exquisite
music of the fraternity has set a gold cage
about each singer. The lyric laws of this
tradition exclude open-air sounds, and all
the world is curtained off in order to seclude
a particular kind of throb.

The tyranny of literary convention is
known to every writer. If he will translate
Homer into Shakespearian blank verse, he
must throw in a little Shakespearian bombast, or the verse will balk like an underfed
horse. If he will put Horace into the Spenserian stanza, he must dose it somewhat
with Elizabethan ornament. Indeed, he
cannot help doing so. The excessive ar-
tificiality of the ancestral school of verse to
which Murray belongs, and of which he is
a sincere exponent, could not help dyeing
Murray's paraphrases of Greek texts in the
blood of Shelley. "What better tint could
he put on?" you cry. Yes, yes; but the
Greek is lost.

Let us take an example. It was Robert
Browning who first cast "God" into British
Victorian poetry,—"God" as a sort of pig-
ment or colophon; "God" as an exclamation,

a parenthesis, an adverb, a running comment, an exordium, a thesis, and a conclusion. Murray inherits this idiosyncrasy: he has taken it in with his poetic milk. One is tempted to write "Browning" against many a page of Murray's *Euripides*.

So far as religion is concerned, the Greeks do seem upon occasion to have dealt with an idea which is best rendered by our word "God." It is an idea that does not occur often in Greek, although there is hardly a page of Greek poetry without some reference to the unseen agency of spirits,— *a* god, *some* god, *the* gods, fate, chance, destiny, etc. In the older literal translations of Greek poetry into English the word "God" seems to be avoided altogether, and "Jove" is used for "Zeus." In the more recent literal translations the name of God is not altogether omitted. For instance, in Coleridge's translation of Euripides' *Medea,* the word occurs half a dozen times, chiefly in phrases such as "God grant," "so help me God," "by God's grace," etc. Willamovitz, the great German scholar, uses the word "Gott," so far as I can find, only twice in his poetic version of *Medea—i.e.,* "Will's Gott" and "Behüt' Euch Gott." In Murray's translation of the same play "God" occurs forty-three times, not counting *"the* god," *"a* god," etc. Such dealing destroys the Greek atmosphere. Horace in Spenserian verse would be Roman compared to this.

There is, however, a further and very mysterious phenomenon connected with Murray's metrical transcriptions. They are accompanied by prefaces and notes in the style of the Oxfordian *littérateurs* of forty years ago. His verse vehicle has for the nonce keeled the whole man over into mawkish cultivation. It is incredible, and a paradox in psychology, that Murray the scholar should have penned these notes.

The ingenuous young student who should look into Euripides himself after reading Murray's translations and introductions to the poet would experience very much such a surprise as a boy does who finds a snake in a bird's nest. The two creatures have nothing to do with each other, except that under certain circumstances the one devours the other,—that is to say, the sceptic devours the sentimentalist.

The purpose of the following pages is to protect that ingenuous boy, to point out some extravagances of this intricate world, and to prepare the good youth of America for the complications of European cultivation.

# GREEK GENIUS

The relation between Euripides and Murray is not a thing that needs to be treated *in extenso,* as, for instance, by comparing everything that the one has said about the other. The question is one of transfusion, of chemical transformation. It can be studied by samples and piecemeal. The discussion requires merely the examination of elements which never vary. For purposes of convenience I shall take up Murray's translation of the *Bacchantes,* because that play is in itself so very remote from British feeling that the divagations of the translator and commentator are brought into picturesque and startling contrast with the Greek. The sentimentalism of this British school when it fondles Greek intellect is like Agave with the head of Pentheus in her arms.

To the poet Murray, Euripides is a misunderstood man who wrote his *Bacchantes* to express a philosophic faith. Euripides was, it appears, living in Macedonia in exile at the time, and was rejoicing over his escape from his enemies. In the volume entitled *Euripides* (Longmans, Green, 1912), Murray, after describing the cult of Dionysus, says:

[110]

# EURIPIDES AND GREEK GENIUS

"The Bacchanals in this play worshipped him [Dionysus] by his many names:

'Iacchos, Bromios, Lord,
God of God born'; and all the mountain felt
And worshipped with them, and the wild
    things knelt,
And ramped and gloried, and the wilderness
Was filled with moving voices and dim
    stress.

That is the kind of god he [Euripides] cele-brates." (Introductory Essay, p. lx.)

Murray continues on a later page:

"Could not the wise men of Athens un-derstand what a child feels, what a wild beast feels, what a poet feels, that to live— to live in the presence of Nature, of Dawn and Sunset, of eternal mysteries and discov-eries and wonders—is in itself a joyous thing?

" 'Love thou the day and night,' he says in another place. 'It is only so that Life can be made what it really is, a Joy: by loving not only your neighbour—he is so vivid an element in life that, unless you do love him, he will spoil all the rest!—but the actual

[ 111 ]

details and processes of living.' Life becomes like the voyage of Dionysus himself over magic seas, or rather, perhaps, like the more chequered voyage of Shelley's lovers:

'While Night
And Day, and Storm and Calm pursue their
flight,
Our ministers across the boundless sea,
Treading each other's heels unheededly'—

the alternations and pains being only 'ministers' to the great composite joy.

"It seemed to Euripides, in that favourite metaphor of his, which was always a little more than a metaphor, that a God had been rejected by the world that he came from. Those haggard, striving, suspicious men, full of ambition and the pride of intellect, almost destitute of emotion,—unless political hatreds can be called emotion,—were hurrying through Life in the presence of august things which they never recognised, of joy and beauty which they never dreamed of. Thus it is that 'the world's wise are not wise.'

" . . . It is a mysticism which includes democracy as it includes the love of your neighbour. They are both necessary details

in the inclusive end. It implies that trust in
the 'simple man' which is so characteristic
of most idealists and most reformers. It
implies the doctrine of Equality—a doctrine
essentially religious and mystical, continu-
ally disproved in every fresh sense in which
it can be formulated, and yet remaining one
of the living faiths of men." (*Ib.*, p. lxiii
*et seq.*)

Now let the ingenuous stripling from
Oshkosh whose father has saved money to
send him to college in New Haven, and who
finds Murray's *Euripides* on the list of
books to be read, try to connect this exquisite kissing of his three fingers by an
Oxford professor with anything that can be
found in the poetry of Euripides, or in any
other Greek thing whatever. What cue has
the boy to the mystery? What aid towards
its solution can he find in the pages of the
old Attic artist, who is more addicted to setting riddles than to solving them?

Murray's state of mind at such moments
cannot be reached by any intellectual appeal.
No matter what button is touched, the same
bell rings. "It is," he says, "a dangerous
and somewhat vulgar course to deduce from
a poet's works direct conclusions about his

[113]

real life." No sooner has he said this than he proceeds to deduce the most recondite conclusions as to the poet's private life from verses which suggest nothing personal. Euripides, according to Murray, "felt like a hunted animal escaped from its pursuers, like a fawn fled to the forest, says one lyric in which the personal note is surely audible as a ringing undertone (l. 862):

'Oh, feet of a fawn to the greenwood fled,
    Alone in the grass and the loveliness,
Leap of the hunted, no more in dread' . . .

"But there is still a terror in the distance behind him; he must go onward yet, to lonely regions where no voice of either man or hound may reach." (*Ib.*, p. lxi.)

That leaping fawn was the call of the wild to Murray. He throws his principles of criticism to the wind, because he has seen an opportunity of winding his own peculiar note on his own elfin horn. As a matter of fact, leaping animals and darting birds were almost a specialty of Euripides, even before his banishment. He must surely have loved wild animals, and he certainly knew the value of them in a chorus; but no one except

[114]

a wizard could guess in which of his animal similes Euripides was describing himself.

I shall now take up some passages from the same Introductory Essay in which Professor Murray points out things of importance which are to be found in the work itself. I begin with a passage in which Murray wilfully perverts the Greek meaning.

" 'What else is wisdom?' Euripides asks in a marvellous passage:

'What else is wisdom? What of man's
    endeavour
Or God's high grace so lovely and so
    great?
To stand from fear set free, to breathe
    and wait;
To hold a hand uplifted over Hate;
And shall not loveliness be loved for-
    ever?'

"He [Euripides] was escaped and happy; he was beyond the reach of Hate."

This certainly is a marvellous find, and drives us to the original. The words, it appears, are part of a chorus sung immediately after Pentheus has gone forth to his death (1. 877). A close translation is as follows:

"Ah! What is wisdom (*i.e.*, man's wit)? What fairer boon hath God given mortals than to raise the hand in victory o'er the foe? What is fair is loved forever."

The note in Mr. Beckwith's school edition says:

"Moral greatness with the ancient Greeks consisted no less in an immutable hatred towards foes than in a constant love towards friends."

The last words, "What is honourable is always pleasant," were, it seems, a proverb.

The 'marvellous passage' cited by Murray is, in fact, a curse by the Chorus, and the curse is repeated, word for word, being sung twice for the sake of emphasis. Does Gilbert Murray believe that the Greek text here will bear his interpretation? The savagery of the Chorus in the *Bacchantes* is horrible, but it is extremely Hellenic; and it is, one might say, the mainspring of the play. Murray's translation is not a translation, not a transcription nor a rendering of any sort, but a flat denial of the original and the insertion of the opposite sentiment in the mouth of the character. Can this be justified? Of course, with metrical translations an immense license is necessary if the translator is to do anything poetic. But has the translator a right to make up *something else* and then say he found it in the original?

The poet Murray must have puzzled for some time over this text before finding his message in it. At last he perceives that by introverting the sense of it something can be done. He adjusts the *sordino,* and, as the melancholy Jaques would say, he draws the *Oxford* out of it as a weasel sucks an egg. But he stops not here. The mood of inspiration is on him. He proceeds to work the passage up into a *Selbstportrait* of Euripides, and to represent the old poet as blessing his enemies from the serenity of his retreat in Macedonia.

Let us now take up two passages in which Murray has introduced modern theological ideas. "Nay, he [Euripides]," says Murray, "was safe, and those who hated him were suffering. A judgment seemed to be upon them, these men who had resolved to have no dealings with 'the three deadly enemies of Empire, Pity and Eloquent Sentiments and the Generosity of Strength'; who lived, as Thucydides says in another passage (vi, 90), in dreams of wider and wider conquest, —the conquest of Sicily, of South Italy, of Carthage and all her Empire, of every country that touched the sea. They had forgotten the essence of religion, forgotten the eternal laws, and the judgment in wait for those who 'worship the Ruthless Will'; who dream

> 'Dreams of the proud man, making great
>     And greater ever
> Things that are not of God.'

"It is against the essential irreligion implied in these dreams that he appeals in the same song:

> 'And is thy faith so much to give?
>     Is it so hard a thing to see,
>     That the Spirit of God, whate'er it be,
> The Law that abides and falters not, ages
>         long,
> The Eternal and Nature-born—these
>         things be strong?' "

Now, as to the "dreams of the proud man," etc. A close translation of the sentence in which the words occur is as follows:

"The might of God moves slowly, yet is

it sure. It punishes those who honour the senseless pride of men, and alike those who, distraught in mind, exalt not the things of God."

With regard to the verse, "And is thy faith so much to give?" etc., a close translation is as follows:

"Man shall not press thought or act beyond the law. 'Tis little to give—the faith that the power divine, whate'er it be, that which ages long have stablished and which is born of nature's law—that this hath strength."

In translating these last two passages Professor Murray has given the sense of the passages, except for the theology implied in the capital letters. We next come to a case that looks like criminal misrepresentation of the Greek meaning.

"In one difficult and beautiful passage," says Murray, "Euripides seems to give us his own apology:

'Knowledge, we are not foes!
 I seek thee diligently;
But the world with a great wind blows,
 Shining, and not from thee;

Blowing to beautiful things,
  On amid dark and light,
Till Life through the trammellings
  Of Laws that are not the Right,
Breaks, clean and pure, and sings,
  Glorying to God in the height!'

"One feels grateful for that voice from the old Euripides amid the strange, new tones of the *Bacchæ*."

Now it appears that this 'difficult and beautiful' passage is a well known corrupt text (l. 1005), one of those choral inheritances where the general meaning is clear but the text, through the errors of copyists, has become hopeless and irrecoverable. Mr. A. H. Cruickshank, in his school edition of the Clarendon Press Series, gives alternate translations, whose differences depend on suggested changes in the text. I copy them both, as they illustrate the difficulties of the subject. Mr. Cruickshank is obliged to make use of paraphrases and of expansions in order to get anything like a clear meaning from the passage. He first translates it as follows:

"I do not rejoice pursuing wisdom, so as to offend the gods, but (I do rejoice pursuing) the other things, great and illustrious, things of a class which ever tend to what is noble,—namely, to lead a pious and pure life day and night."

His second translation is as follows:

"I envy not (false) wisdom, but I rejoice pursuing those other matters, which are manifestly important, ever leading life to noble ends,—namely, that a man should day and night be pious and holy, and honour the gods by rejecting all the ordinances that are beyond the pale of justice."

Considering the darkness which broods over this particular passage, it might seem disingenuous in Murray to translate the passage as he has done, ending up with: "Glorying to God in the height!",—*and then add:* "One feels grateful for that voice from the old Euripides amid the strange, new tones of the *Bacchæ.*" But it is not disingenuous; it is the very reverse: it is ingenuous, most ingenuous. The Neo-Hellene of Oxford regards a Greek play as a bundle of Sibylline leaves blown wildly about a cavern. The prophetess thrusts one of them into the scholar's hand, and he sings. To the Neo-Hellene a Greek dramatist is a moody, groping sort of person who lives in a maze of intimations,—intimations of Oxford,—and commits almost anything to paper that passes through his head. Says Murray in this same Introductory Essay:

"Probably all dramatists who possess strong personal beliefs yield at times to the temptation of using one of their characters as a mouthpiece for their own feelings. And the Greek Chorus, a half-dramatic, half-lyrical creation, both was, and was felt to be, particularly suitable for such use. Of course a writer does not—or at least should not—use the drama to express his mere 'views' on ordinary and commonplace questions, to announce his side in politics or his sect in religion. But it is a method wonderfully contrived for expressing those vaguer faiths and aspirations which a man feels haunting him and calling to him, but which he cannot state in plain language or uphold with a full acceptance of responsibility. You can say the thing that wishes to be said; you 'give it its chance'; you relieve your mind of it. And if it proves to be all nonsense—well, it is not you that said it. It is

only a character in one of your plays!"
(*Ib.,* p. lviii.)

It would be difficult to say anything more
misleading than this about the Greek theatre,
where every word was a stone in the arch of
the play, every character was provided by
tradition, every thought was conventional.
The structural nature of a Greek drama is
known to everyone, and is perfectly well
known to Mr. Gilbert Murray; but the
fumes from his tripod cover his brain as he
writes his translations, and these fumes per-
vade the introductions and the notes to the
poems. The merit of the verse itself is due
to this very envelope of steaming inspiration and poetic sentiment. But the waking
Murray ought really to join in warning the
public against the hymning, dreamy, irre-
sponsible Murray, the poet Murray who is
spreading grotesque ideas about Euripides
beneath every shaded lamp in the Anglo-
Saxon world.

We are thus compelled, then, to look
askance at one very visible and very charming branch of Greek scholarship at Oxford,
and to sink new foundations of our own, if
we would escape the cloying influence of this
literary school. Perhaps there is not any-

thing novel or anything very desperate in
such a situation. The tendency of universities has ever been to breed cliques and secret
societies, to produce embroideries and start
hothouses of specialised feeling. They do
well in doing this: it is all they can do. We
should look upon them as great furnaces of
culture, largely social in their influence,
which warm and nourish the general temperament of a nation.

Would that in America we had a local
school of classic cultivation half as interesting as this Neo-Hellenism of Oxford,
quaint and non-intellectual as it is! It is
alive and it is national. While most absurd
from the point of view of universal culture,
it is most satisfactory from the domestic
point of view,—as, indeed, everything in
England is. If in America we shall ever
develop any true universities, they will have
faults of their own. Their defects will be
of a new strain, no doubt, and will reflect
our national shortcomings. These thoughts
but teach us that we cannot use other people's eyes or other people's eye-glasses. We
have still to grind the lenses through which
we shall, in our turn, observe the classics.

# VII

## CONCLUSION

THERE is one thing that we should never do in dealing with anything Greek. We should not take a scrap of the Greek mind and keep on examining it until we find a familiar thought in it. No bit of Greek art is to be viewed as a thing in itself. It is always a fragment, and gets its value from the whole. Every bit of carved stone picked up in Athens is a piece of architecture; so is every speech in a play, every phrase in a dialogue. You must go back and bring in the whole Theatre or the whole Academy, and put back the fragment in its place by means of ladders, before you can guess at its meaning. The inordinate significance that seems to gleam from every broken toy of Greece results from this very quality,—that the object is a part of something else. Just because the thing has no meaning by itself, it implies so much. Somehow it drags the whole life of the Greek nation before you. The favourite Greek maxim, "Avoid excess," does the same. It keeps telling you to remember yesterday and to-morrow; to remember the *palæstra* and the market-place; above all, to remember that the very opposite of what you say is also true. Wherever you are, and whatever doing, you must remember the *rest* of the Greek world.

It is no wonder that the Greeks could not adopt the standards and contrivances of other nations, while their own standards and contrivances resulted from such refined and perpetual balancing and shaving of values. This refinement has become part of their daily life; and whether one examines a drinking-cup or a dialogue or a lyric, and whether the thing be from the age of Homer or from the age of Alexander, the fragment always gives us a glimpse into the same Greek world. The foundation of this world seems to be the Myth; and as the world grew it developed in terms of Myth. The Greek mind had only one background. Athletics and Statuary, Epic and Drama, Religion and Art, Scepticism and Science, expressed themselves through the same myths. In this lies the fascination of Greece for us. What a complete cosmos it is! And how different from any other civilisation! Modern life, like modern language, is a monstrous amalgam, a conglomeration and mess of idioms from every age and every clime. The classic Greek hangs together like a wreath. It has been developed rapidly, during a few hundred years, and has an inner harmony like the temple. Language and temple,—each was an apparition; each is, in its own way, perfect.

Consider wherein Rome differed from Greece. The life of the Romans was a patchwork, like our own. Their religion was formal, their art imported, their literature imitative; their aims were practical, their interests unimaginative. All social needs were controlled by political considerations. This sounds almost like a description of modern life, and it explains why the Romans are so close to us. Cicero, Horace, Cæsar, Antony, are moderns. But Alcibiades, Socrates, Pericles, and the rest take their stand in Greek fable. Like Pisistratus, Solon, and Lycurgus, they melt into legend and belong to the realms of the imagination.

No other people ever bore the same relation to their arts that the Greeks bore; and in this lies their charm. When the Alexandrine critics began to classify poetry and to discuss perfection, they never even mentioned the Roman poetry, although all of the greatest of it was in existence. Why is this? It is because no Roman poem is a poem at all from the Greek point of view. It is too individual, too clever, and, generally, too political. Besides, it is not in Greek. The nearest modern analogy to the development of the whole Greek world of art is to be found in German contrapuntal music. No one except a German has ever written a true sonata or a symphony in the true polyphonic German style. There are *tours de force* done by other nationalities, but the natural idiom of this music is Teutonic.

I am not condemning the Latins or the moderns. Indeed, there is in Horace something nobler and more humane than in all Olympus. The Greeks, moreover, seem in their civic incompetence like children when contrasted with the Romans or with the moderns. But in power of utterance, within their own crafts, the Greeks are unapproachable. Let us now speak of matters of which we know very little.

The statues on the Parthenon stand in a region where direct criticism cannot reach them, but which trigonometry may, to some extent, determine. Their beauty probably

results from an artistic knowledge so refined, a sophistication so exact, that, as we
gaze, we lose the process and see only results.
A Greek architect could have told you just
what lines of analysis must be followed in
order to get these effects in grouping and in
relief. It is all, no doubt, built up out of
*tonic* and *dominant,* but the manual of
counterpoint has been lost. As the tragic
poet fills the stage with the legend, so the
sculptor fills the metope with the legend.
Both are closely following artistic usage :
each is merely telling the old story with new
refinement. And whether we gaze at the
actors on the stage or at the figures in the
metope, whether we study a lyric or listen to
a dialogue, we are in communion with the
same genius, the same legend. The thing
which moves and delights us is a unity.

This Genius is not hard to understand.
Anyone can understand it. That is the
proof of its greatness. As Boccaccio said of
Dante, not learning but good wits are needed
to appreciate him. One cannot safely look
towards the mind of the modern scholar for
an understanding of the Greek mind, because
the modern scholar is a specialist, a thing
the Greek abhors. If a scholar to-day knows
the acoustics of the Greek stage, that is

thought to be a large enough province for him. He is not allowed to be an authority on the scenery. In the modern scholar's mind everything is in cubby-holes; and everybody to-day wants to become an authority. Everyone, moreover, is very serious to-day; and it does not do to be too serious about Greek things, because the very genius of Greece has in it a touch of irony which combines with our seriousness to make a heavy, indigestible paste. The Greek will always laugh at you if he can, and the only hope is to keep him at arm's length and deal with him in the spirit of social life, of the world, of the *beau monde,* and of large conversation. His chief merit is to stimulate this spirit. The less we dogmatise about his works and ways, the freer will the world be of secondary, second-rate commentaries. The more we study his works and ways, the fuller will the world become of intellectual force.

The Greek classics are a great help in tearing open those strong envelopes in which the cultivation of the world is constantly getting glued up. They helped Europe to cut free from theocratic tyranny in the late Middle Ages. They held the Western world together after the fall of the Papacy.

# EURIPIDES AND GREEK GENIUS

They gave us modern literature: indeed, if one considers all that comes from Greece, one can hardly imagine what the world would have been like without her. The lamps of Greek thought are still burning in marble and in letters. The complete little microcosm of that Greek society hangs forever in the great macrocosm of the moving world, and sheds rays which dissolve prejudice, making men thoughtful, rational, and gay. The greatest intellects are ever the most powerfully affected by it; but no one escapes. Nor can the world ever lose this benign influence, which must, so far as philosophy can imagine, qualify human life forever.

# II

# SHAKESPEARE

# I

## THE GREEK STAGE AND SHAKESPEARE

THE classic stage and Shakespeare's theatre have, at first sight, nothing in common; for the first was dedicated to unity, the second to variety. The great size of the antique stage made unity essential. A play had but three or four characters and involved but one or two ideas, which were hammered upon during the entire performance. When the heroes ceased speaking, the Chorus took up the thread of the argument. A Greek tragedy, moreover, was of national origin and of religious import. The plot was always taken from a familiar myth; and only great personages, heroes, kings and princes, were allowed upon the stage.

A play of Shakespeare's, on the other hand, was acted in a small space, and involved twenty or thirty characters. It took place amid hurried shiftings of scene (imaginary scene, for there was next to no real scenery). The plot was any story under the

sun.  Tragedy and comedy were mixed.  It
had no public or religious significance.  In
fact, it was always on the verge of being
taboo, and was constantly told by the
police to move on.  As for unity and the
Unities, the fixed and stationary character
of the staging itself was about the only unity
in many Elizabethan plays.

In spite of these vast differences between
the Greek stage and Shakespeare's stage,
there are certain resemblances between the
greatest of Shakespeare's tragedies and the
greatest Greek tragedies.  There is, in a few
of Shakespeare's plays, as in *Othello* and
*King Lear,* a unity of theme, a single moving column of idea, which makes them
analogous to Greek plays, though all the
machinery is different.  Then the language
of Shakespeare's loftiest tragic vein has
many turns of thought and metaphor which
are surprisingly like the Greek.  Then, too,
both theatres are intellectual,—that is to say,
the appeal is an intellectual appeal, done
through the presentation of ideas in the text,
not through melodrama or pantomime.
Every idea is articulated into words.  If a
person has a pain or sees someone coming he
says: "I have a pain," "I see someone coming."  The thoughts and purposes of the

# SHAKESPEARE

characters are thus metaphysically presented, and are often expounded with a rhetorical power which the stage functions of the characters do not suggest. Both on the Greek and on the English stage each character has, as it were, the privilege of becoming the poet; and it is the unspoken convention that no one shall notice the excursion. There is a danger connected with this privilege; for when the poet gets on his own hobby he is apt to make the little fishes talk like whales. For instance, it is natural that an old nurse should talk about death and the next world; but it is not natural that an old nurse should betray the peculiar cast of thought of a philosophic scholar, which Euripides throws over Phædra's attendant. The old woman closes a philosophic speech as follows: "And so we show our mad love of this life because its light is shed on earth, and because we know no other, and have naught revealed to us of all our Earth may hide; and trusting to fables, we drift at random."

So also Shakespeare, in *As You Like It*, suddenly endows Phœbe the shepherdess with a "discourse of reason" much resembling Hamlet's, because a subject has come up that interests the poet,—namely, the

[137]

difference between physical injury and mental distress.

"Lean but upon a rush," says Phœbe,
"The cicatrice and capable impressure
 Thy palm some moment keeps, but now
     mine eyes,
 Which I have darted at thee, hurt thee
     not."

It is the blank verse that gives the nurse and Phœbe this enlargement of their powers. In fact, both Greek tragedy and Shakespearian tragedy are in their poetic march a sort of great Gargantuan discourse issuing from the mouth of the poet, the stage being his jaws.

There is yet another resemblance between Shakespeare and the Greeks. Both the Greek tragedies and Shakespeare's best plays have been written with supreme facility. They have fallen from the pen. They exist in a region of artistic fulfilment. I suspect that it is this latter element of perfection that links Shakespeare and the Greeks in our thought, rather than all the rest of their scanty resemblances. So far as perfection of form goes, the Greek plays are infinitely superior to Shakespeare's. So far as native

talent goes, there is no Greek dramatist who
stands anywhere near Shakespeare, though
Aristophanes suggests him. In each case
perfection reaches a climax. With the
Greeks it is the perfection of massive racial
power; with Shakespeare, the perfection of
modern romantic sentiment.

## II

THE invention of the alphabet very soon turned all forms of articulate expression into mere reading and writing. The first edition of Homer's poems, no doubt, threw the reciters out of work, and handed over the poems bound hand and foot to the literary fraternity,—to those men with ink-bottles and sheets of parchment who have owned and controlled the poems ever since. (Happy is the ordinary man if the scholars will give him but a peep at them!) To-day we have almost forgotten that Homer was originally intended for recitation, not for reading. The form in which we know the Iliad is due, thinks Professor Gilbert Murray, to the demands of a *reading* public. In like manner, Shakespeare's plays have, during the last two hundred years, been kept upon the stage largely through the influence of the reading public. The world will un-

[141]

doubtedly continue to read the plays long after they have ceased to walk the boards.

There is a great and terrible truth at the bottom of this outcome. Things are better understood, more rapidly and more vividly taken in, when they are read than when they are recited or acted; and though the rise of a great actor may now and then qualify this rule for a day, though Garrick or Edmund Kean or Salvini may show the true Shakespeare in a flash, the memory of which lasts for the hearer's lifetime, yet the mass of men must depend on the printed page for all their knowledge of Homer or of Shakespeare. We know *Hamlet* so well that it is only by an effort that we remember that *Hamlet* was once a play, a thing unfamiliar, a novelty in a theatre, where people sat and wondered and watched the actors. Shakespeare on the stage has been murdered by Shakespeare in the closet. The theatre of one's own mind is more interesting than any actual theatre, and our inward actors outdo all but the greatest tragedians and comedians of the world.

On the real stage things move too slowly. I am bored with every speech: the lines are too familiar. The theatre compels me to take in the text by linear measurement, and

[142]

never to skip. I cannot turn the page or dwell upon a favourite passage. I am cramped and bullied and held in place. And, after all, what do I get in a theatre that cannot be got in the easy-chair, where all the actors become brilliant and the plot never lags?

We need not wonder, then, that the literary influences, the pen-and-ink, closet influences of the world have controlled Homer and Æschylus, for we see that they control Shakespeare. There is hardly a student of the poet, there is hardly a commentator on him, who thinks of the stage once in a volume; and worst of all,—most dreadful of all,—Shakespeare himself forgets the stage for hours together. He becomes so inward, so excited, so inwound in his own enchantments that much of his greatest thought is lost in the staging of it. He is more poet than dramatist. He is the victim and the archangel of pen and ink.

Nevertheless, in reviewing Shakespeare one must go back to the Globe Theatre and to those other murky jars out of which the clouds issued that have filled the world. The little tumbledown barns where his plays were staged, and the ragged succession of scenes that constituted a drama in his day,

required variety and rapid handling. Shades
of humour and of extravagance abound;
parenthetical, non‑dramatic, personal
touches, things which come from nowhere
and vanish. They abound because the au‑
dience is close to the actors and can enjoy
them. The boards are flooded by a con‑
course of characters, comic and tragic.
There is an interweaving of several plots,
no division into acts, a swarming of hu‑
manity as at a fair, and generally no scenic
interest, no *pièce montée* at the end. A play
ends where it ends, often with only two per‑
sons on the stage. Instead of the "features"
of the classic stage,—I mean the well‑under‑
stood, artistic members of a Greek play, as
the recitations by messengers, dramatic
dialogues, trochaic passages, etc.,—we have
improvised features of Shakespeare's own
invention, bits of ornament thrown in as it
strikes his fancy to use them; as, for in‑
stance, Jaques' "Seven Ages," Mercutio's
"Queen Mab," Hamlet's "Speech to the
Players," Lorenzo's "On Such a Night as
this." There are also ornamental character‑
isations, as, for instance, Queen Katherine's
character of Wolsey, Iago's satirical sketch
of the "Perfect Woman,"—moral saws, and
bits of description, sometimes raised through

SHAKESPEARE

the alchemy of inspiration into the greatest
poetry in existence. All these things are
flung and sowed along the path of the play
and distract us into little unexpected palaces
of happiness.

The dramatic practices of Shakespeare
and of his contemporaries can hardly be
called a school of drama. What other man
except Shakespeare could succeed in his
method of play-writing? It is the Elizabethan method; but there was only one
Elizabethan who could write thus and be
readable or actable. The rest of them have
been dragged into nineteenth-century notice
by the archæologists of literature, but are
about to fall back into the limbo where they
belong. It is all a personal charm, this
charm of Shakespeare's, and criticism can
no more reach the essence of it than we can
define the smell of a rose. It is in each
phrase that the mystery lies. The poet himself was unconscious and indifferent as to
the whole phenomenon of his talent; and
we are likelier to reach him if we follow him
in this very indifference than if we attempt
an analysis. The Greeks were critics by
nature, and we may sauce them with their
own polite learning without fear of becoming ridiculous; but the academic person has

never been quite able to get Shakespeare into his *palazzo*. He tries to introduce the poet through the front portico; but the columns are too close together. Then he leads him round to the back, takes down part of the wall, and so leaves our poet in the back yard, not omitting, however, to put up a fine inscription about him in the rotunda. The truth is that the philosophical machinery of Learning does not help us here. We are more apt to take a good observation of Shakespeare by lying in the grass and making a guess than by erecting a telescope. As to Shakespeare's art and his technique, the critics have been at work over them for a hundred years, and have found him to be a master of the craft of his own kind of stage, whenever he chose to be such. We need not dispute this: it is a small part of the subject. Nevertheless, Shakespeare's stage technique is as experimental as the rest of his work. He has no system, but only habits; and these habits hang so loosely on him that very often he forgets where he is, and does something unexpected.

The plays were certainly meant for rapid presentation. It is impossible to recite Hamlet's advice to the players in an ordinary modern theatre without violating every

injunction of the poet as to proper diction
and delivery. If you follow Hamlet's in-
junctions, the speech will not be heard or
understood by a third of your modern audience. *King Lear* cannot be staged—it is
too long—unless the actors crowd on and
off the boards like the characters in the
greenroom of a circus. No one of us has
ever seen a Shakespeare play given as it
ought to be given; for traditional acting has
put *intention* into everything; pauses, elocu-
tion and eye-work are *de rigueur;* the vanity
of a dozen generations of actors has trained
the public to expect, not a play, but selected
scenes from Shakespeare, well dressed up
and painstakingly interpreted.

The *forte* of the small theatre is that it
can make passing allusions to vivid personal
traits. Shakespeare's plays are full of characters that remind us of Teniers and of
Rembrandt. It is a stage where fleeting
imaginative impressions chase one another,
and nothing is monumental. It is like the
internal stage of the mind. It is, in fact, the
stage of Shakespeare's own mind, almost
unsubdued to reality, unvisited by the stage
carpenter. This is the most internal writing
ever done, this writing of Shakespeare's; it
is like the writing of a man in a dream. The

critics since Coleridge have found "intention" and "judgment" and "calculation" of
all sorts in Shakespeare; and Professor A.
C. Bradley finds that the intricacies of logic
and motive in *Othello* have been studied and
thought out. Ah, no! they have never been
studied; they have been improvised with the
lightning (and sometimes with the thunder
and lightning) of genius; but it is all improvisation, it is the making of a charade
for a night's phantasy. The great charm of
it all comes from Shakespeare's self, and
cannot be reduced to dramatic elements.

The great power of Shakespeare is that he
loves his characters. This is the persistent
force that holds us. No creator has ever
loved his creatures so much as Shakespeare
has loved these characters. This is the cable
that draws us. Next to this, and perhaps co-
equal with it in power, is the hidden chain of
contemplation that runs invisible and courses
at the back of each play. One of the greatest thinkers that ever lived is in action. He
does not know that he is thinking; he is
merely recording thoughts that arise in him.
On these two threads of a continuous
benevolence and a consecutive course of
thought Shakespeare hangs one dramatic
device after another, so various and so bril-

liant that we have the drama, as it were, thrown in; we have flashes and abysses of drama,—more than we bargained for. Shakespeare is a dramatist, fifty kinds of a dramatist all at once; but the drama is only a small part of Shakespeare's mind.

There is one light in which Shakespeare is unique: he is gay. He is the only great poet who is gay; for Homer and Dante are sombre. Pure happiness is the rarest thing in poetry. You may search the collections of excerpts not quite in vain for a verse here and there that is not sad; but poetic sentiment is traditionally and habitually gloomy. Yet open Shakespeare, and you almost always open upon redundant, shining happiness.

Perhaps in studying the Shakespearian drama one ought to begin with the chronicle-plays; for this was where Shakespeare himself began. A cycle of historic dramas was in existence before Shakespeare appeared. The old chronicle-play is a key to what the Elizabethan public expected and enjoyed. The interest in the whole lay in the staging of certain familiar heroes and kings, who are engaged in picturesque, martial and political imbroglios. It was a Homeric sort of appeal that drew people to these shows,

Talbot and Joan of Arc and the procession
of old English kings were images in the
public mind.

In the process of making this old drama
more interesting, Shakespeare made it more
coherent. It was a decorative, popular,
moving panorama of bombast, into which
he threw every kind of genius. If you take
his series of historical plays, from *Henry
VI*, through *King John, Richard II, Richard III, Henry IV, Henry V,* and *Henry
VIII*, they seem like a splendid set of
tapestries. The later plays are more dramatically articulated, and much more brilliant in every way, than the earlier ones; yet
their appeal remains plastic or Homeric
rather than dramatic. The fate-motive
which flickers in and out among the historical plays was dealt with lightly, except
in *Richard III,* where it took the centre of
the stage and gave to that play its early and
enduring popularity. On the whole, however, we must think of the single scene as
the dramatic unit in this kind of drama.
Each play strives to stage a set of stirring
episodes rather than a story. The playwright presents street fights, small proces-
sions, alarums, people carried on the stage
in arm-chairs to die (the first inventor of

this feature must have made a hit!),
proclamations, defiances, magniloquent dec-
lamations, cursings, boastings, tumults, and
any excuse for a rumpus on the stage. All
this is the raw material out of which Shakespeare evolved his art.

If you read a few of the stage directions
in *Henry VI,* they will give the *milieu* of the
old chronicle-play:

"The Same Before the Gates. Skirmish-
ings. Talbot pursues the Dauphin, drives
him in, and exit; then enter Joan La Pucelle,
driving Englishmen before her, and exit
after them. Then re-enter Talbot." Again:
"Enter Talbot, Bedford, Burgundy and
Forces, with scaling-ladders, their drums
beating a dead march." Again: "The
French leap over the walls in their shirts,"
etc.

The rapidity of Shakespeare's development is the startling part of him. For if
*Henry VI* is Giotto, *Henry IV* is Michelan-
gelo and Paul Veronese. The immense
license of the Elizabethan stage was what
Shakespeare needed; and out of it he grew,
unchastened, unconscious of boundary or
law, ever pursuing his latest thought. The

power that descended upon him was a power of coherent excitement, which came and went at its own will. He seems not to have known the difference between writing with inspiration and writing without inspiration. Other poets have lived in a like ignorance of their own moods. Wordsworth, for instance, passed from divinity to dulness without being aware of it. The difference between the two men is that Wordsworth believed that all he wrote was inspired; whereas Shakespeare apparently regarded all his own compositions as a harmless kind of rubbish.

In Shakespeare's case the poet was subject to so many kinds of inspiration that when one stopped, another was apt to begin; and we ourselves who read him are whirled away with the new force, not knowing where we are or how we are being dealt with. In the play of *King John* the story proceeds at a jog-trot till the scene in which King John instructs Hubert to kill little Prince Arthur. Here for one moment there falls on the scene an immense seriousness, like a blast out of *Macbeth:*

*King.* Thou art his keeper.
*Hubert.*　　　　　　And I'll keep him so,

# SHAKESPEARE

That he shall not offend your majesty.
*King.*                                    Death.
*Hubert.*   My lord.
*King.*             A grave.
*Hubert.*                 He shall not live.
*King.*                           Enough.
    I could be merry now.   Hubert, I love
       thee;
    Well, I'll not say what I intend for thee:
    Remember.   (*To the Queen.*)   Madam,
       fare you well:
    I'll send those powers o'er to your
       majesty.

Again, in the same play, there is a sort of divine beauty in the scene between Hubert and little Arthur; and this in spite of the fact that little Arthur is a monster, not like a boy in the least, and talks as no boy ever talked.   While Shakespeare was writing the historical plays his talent developed rapidly, spontaneously, and in all directions at once. He found himself among hurricanes, and he let them blow; among zephyrs, and he let them breathe or die at their will.   This was ever his way.

In the third act of *Hamlet* a dramatic gust dies out as mysteriously as the strange blast of feeling arises about the little boy in

## GREEK GENIUS

*King John.* From the opening of the play, down to the scene between Hamlet and his mother, we are in the atmosphere of the greatest kind of drama. It is a fate-drama, as powerful as the *Agamemnon* of Æschylus. Our souls are shaken with its reality. This religious interest comes to its climax in Hamlet's sudden vision of the spectre which his mother cannot see. The woman, whose whole heart has been torn to shreds by her son's reproaches, now for a moment forgets everything except her terror in the discovery that Hamlet is really mad. This is a climax out of the supernatural into the natural, such as no one except Shakespeare was ever capable of. The scene is as great as anything in human literature. Then Shakespeare gets tired of the Ghost. He leaves the poor Ghost and his whole story behind, drops it as a dog drops a bone that he has wearied of, and goes gambolling upon the horizon. From this point onward Shakespeare holds the play together with grave-diggers, brilliant soliloquies, young men in frenzy of passion who come to grips over a girl's bier, duels, murders, and a dead march. These latter scenes, however, which are hustled on to the stage, half dressed, to piece out the performance, are as magical as

[154]

the earlier parts of the drama. No wonder
they made Shakespeare forget the Ghost.
Ophelia, with her scraps of lyric phrase
which have the power of Sappho at the back
of them, moves upon our gaze. We receive
dreadful gleams from the mystery behind all
life,—fragments of thought, where the passion of forty Dantes is put into accidents of
phrase. No wonder the Ghost and the whole
plot and scheme of the play were withdrawn
from Shakespeare's mind. He winds all
up with a thoroughgoing Elizabethan hurly-
burly. The main interest, it must be confessed, is never recovered. By the time the
curtain falls in *Hamlet* the characters have
become marionettes. They lie about the
stage, and one hardly knows which is the
king.

All this *finale* of Hamlet is very inartistic.
It certainly would have been easy at least to
introduce the Ghost for a last triumphant,
sorrowing, magnificent speech over the dead
bodies; and this would have tended to pull
the play together. But the Ghost is as far
from Shakespeare's mind as Helen of
Troy, and is almost as completely banished
from the action. What is it, then, that
keeps the audience in the theatre during the
last act of Hamlet? Perhaps it is something

GREEK GENIUS

that cannot be stated or even be clearly imagined.  Yet through it is conveyed the operation of gigantic Mind, which flashes from Shakespeare as he thinks and dreams and proceeds in his extraordinary journey through the play.  It would seem as if all the lighting and staging and arrangements that we have been taught to consider as the essentials of dramatic art are not needed; for Shakespeare produces the most profound effects without any of them.  We cannot find his vehicle.  We are left standing on the edge of the abyss, not knowing how we came there, or we are lulled in the music of Elysium, not knowing why it sounds.

# III

## EACH PLAY A WORLD

THERE is a world in each of Shakespeare's plays,—*the* world, I should say,—so felt and so seen as the world never was seen before nor could be felt and seen again, even by Shakespeare. Each play is a little local universe. His stage devices he repeats, but the atmosphere of a play is never repeated. *Twelfth Night, As You Like It,* and *The Merchant of Venice* are very unlike one another. The unity that is in each of them results from unimaginable depths of internal harmony in each. The group of persons in any play (I am speaking of the good plays) forms the unity; for the characters are psychologically interlocked with one another. Prospero implies Caliban; Toby Belch implies Malvolio; Shylock, Antonio. The effects of all imaginative art result from subtle implications and adjustments. The public recognises these things as beauty, but cannot analyse them.

# GREEK GENIUS

To the artist, however, they have been the
bricks and mortar out of which the work
was builded. We feel, for instance, in the
*Midsummer-Night's Dream,* that the fairies
are somehow correlative to the artisans.
They are made out of a complementary
chemical. On the other hand, Theseus and
Demetrius and Hippolyta, in the same play,
are lay figures which set off as with a foil
both the fairies and the artisans. Theseus,
Hippolyta, and Demetrius are marionettes
which give intellect and importance to Bottom and Flute, and lend body and life to the
tiny fairies. All this miraculous subtlety of
understanding on Shakespeare's part is unconscious. He has had no recipe, no *métier.*

The colouring of each play, its humour,
its mood, is Shakespeare's mood as he wrote
the play. The mood of desperate philosophic
questioning in which he wrote *Hamlet* gives
to the play its only unity. So *Macbeth* and
*King Lear* are each beclouded by its own
kind of passionate speculation. The story is,
in each case, a mere thread to catch the crystals from an overcharged atmosphere of
feeling. The tragedy of *Lear* is loftier,
more abstract in thought, and at the same
time more hotly human in feeling than *Macbeth.* It is in these worlds of mood that we

[ 158 ]

must seek Shakespeare, and we must remain somewhat moody and dreamy ourselves during the search. If we take a pair of tongs to catch him, he will elude us.

In *Othello,* Shakespeare seems to have become interested in working out the destruction of a noble soul by means of a stage demon, a sort of Richard III in private life and without ambition. Iago has no motive, and Othello has no weakness; and the conjunction of the two persons is artificial. The idea is, nevertheless, elaborated with diabolical cunning on the playwright's part, and the picture of Othello remains the best picture of jealousy in literature; so that the play belongs at the head of all problem plays. If considered seriously, *Othello* is a plea for evil; but, properly taken, it is a sort of awful *jeu d'esprit.* An odious play it is, false to life and without overtones. Yet so gigantic is the mind that became interested in this odious problem, and so thoroughly equipped in play-writing, that the world, after three centuries, goes on being deceived and fascinated by the story. Shakespeare's interest in the play is a playwright's interest; and he happens not to weary of the problem or to stray from his main theme during the whole course of the story. *Othello* is like a Greek tragedy in that it is a masterpiece of artificial logic with a bad ending. But, of course, *Othello* is extremely unlike the Greek from every other point of view; as, for instance, it has many characters, a complexity of plot, a shifting of scene, a very hard and non-lyrical treatment, and endless Elizabethan hurly-burly. We must never forget that the radical difference between ancient and modern drama is that modern drama is always unfolding a story. We are kept wondering how the thing will turn out. Ancient drama, on the contrary, takes the plot for granted and focuses our whole attention upon the treatment.

The unexampled spontaneousness of Shakespeare is due to the flame of his own curiosity, that hums like a great fire through his plays, which are plays only incidentally, —they are really studies, the memorandum books of a man who is thinking,—water-colour sketches made by an amateur for his own pleasure, and then filed away never to be examined again. Shakespeare has lived in them as he wrote them; he knows not their limits; he has no intentions, no subsequent curiosity. In spite of their stage merits, they lose by being acted, as things delicate lose by being placarded. Compared to Molière's plays, they show imperfection everywhere. But there is so much genius in them,—as much, perhaps, as there is in the rest of literature outside of them,—that they belong to a superhuman world. No one ever wrote like this before. It is a new vehicle. There exists nothing with which to compare it. There was a good deal of truth in the early view which regarded Shakespeare as a gifted savage. He does not make the compromises or play the game of stage art. But he is following law of some sort, or he could not have become so popular. In multifarious appeal he has no fellow. The child loves his wit, the youth his passion, the middle-aged person his knowledge of the world, the old man his metaphysical power, and all men his benevolence.

What is a play? I do not know; but I am sure that these things are much more than plays: to me they are metaphysical treatises. There never was a creature like Hamlet, and never can be: Hamlet is a philosophical gimcrack. He shows the mind of an elderly man set upon the shoulders of a boy of eighteen, and turned loose in a tragic situation. What a monstrous apparatus of thought is here set up! There never was a man like Macbeth, and there never can be. An over-

sensitive, morbid, middle-aged recluse commits a brutal murder in a barbarous Scotch
castle, and then gives himself the horrors
by plunging about in his double character of
bloody borderer and lyric hypochondriac.
Men are not like that. There never was a
man like Richard III, or indeed like any
other complete stage villain. The stage villain is a comparatively low form of artificial
device. He is a metaphysical hypothesis,
like the rest, invented for purposes of demonstration.

Perhaps we ought, in dealing with this
whole subject, to begin by regarding all
stage-land, from wheels and pulleys to poetic
metaphors, as a congeries of things that are
essentially and necessarily false and make-
believe,—elaborately constructed things,
which, properly used, flash a momentary illusion of truth into the sympathetic eye, but
which will not stand inspection,—no, not
for a moment. The people who write essays
on Shakespeare's characters, treating them
as real, have found a pretty amusement,
which is about as valuable as the literary
pastime of writing imaginary conversations
between famous dead people. A stage character is always merely the fragment of a
picture. Perhaps only a profile is shown;

and yet its duty is done then and there. No more than this profile of the man ever existed, and we can never know what a full view of the face might reveal. If we add to Shakespeare's sketch by tacking on a bit of our own imagination, we shall produce a strange rag doll, just as the writers of imaginary conversations produce strange rag dolls.

When we come to *King Lear* we are in deep waters. In this play the passion and the tragedy develop so naturally, so unexpectedly, and so suddenly out of the halcyon opening of the drama that we are taken unaware. The clouds gather and the lightning plays about, and, lo! we are in the heights and depths of human experience. But how did we get there? What element has done this, and what does it all mean? Shakespeare neither knew nor cared. Hidden within *King Lear,* as in *Hamlet,* is a terrific metaphysical apparatus, a psychometer or dynamo of passion. It sets the machinery of our hearts in motion. The thing has been inserted into our minds and works its own will upon us. The comment, or chorus work, which in *Hamlet* and in *Macbeth* is done by the protagonists themselves, is in *King Lear* distributed to a jester, a pretended madman and a friend in disguise. Lear himself is not a double consciousness like Hamlet or Macbeth, but a passionate, feeble-minded, ignorant old man, who becomes pathetic chiefly through his age. But why is this pathos so deep? And why do the little dogs, Tray, Blanche, and Sweetheart, move us so profoundly? I suppose that Shakespeare himself has been greatly moved as he lived through the scenes in all these plays. He has not known just why the plots worked out as they did. He was evidently experimenting, and found that his themes worked up to these climaxes automatically. In *Timon of Athens* he worries and rages, yet nothing will come of it. In *Coriolanus* he works like a Trojan, and is as dull as Corneille.

If Shakespeare had only been an artist like Leonardo, who was always calculating effects and analysing causes, we might know something of his art. But the fact is that he knew nothing about the matter himself, and does not aid us. He does not know what has happened. Let us take an illustration of his ingenuousness. He reads Montaigne's essay on Sebondus,—that great, long, impassioned essay, in which Montaigne demonstrates the impotency of man,

his inability to know anything whatever, his
helplessness, and the absurdity of all human
pretence to intellect. It is Essay No. XII
in the Second Book, and we can all follow
in Everyman's Library the very text which
Shakespeare pondered. Shakespeare read
this essay with a devouring curiosity, and absorbed its ideas,—which, after all, are ideas
that are never long absent from any thoughtful mind. The *"Que sçai-je?"* of Montaigne might be Shakespeare's own motto,
were not Shakespeare too profoundly unconscious to have any motto. He reads
Montaigne, and for a time he *becomes* Montaigne. For a time he sees the whole universe from the point of view of the sceptic;
and while this influence is upon him he
becomes interested in refurbishing the old
stock play of *Hamlet*. Before he is aware,
he has begun to use Hamlet as a stalking-
horse for Montaigne's philosophy. He does
not invent Hamlet as Goethe invents Mephistopheles. Hamlet is merely the result of
the different problems and occupations of
Shakespeare's private mind. Shakespeare's
primary interest is an interest in life, not an
interest in play-writing or in philosophy;
these things are subsidiary toys, algebraical
signs, to him. And when, as in *Hamlet*, it

turns out that the playwright has made a monster, he never stops to consider the matter. For Shakespeare does not know that his own talent is a talent for thinking, that his own chief interest lies in speculation. He thinks he is telling a story, and he believes that all these ideas are in the story: he sees them in the tale itself.

There are writers who write for themselves. They have a curiosity, they have a passion for study and for statement, and a joy in the process of writing. Their writings are personal memoirs. Saint-Simon and Samuel Pepys are men of genius by reason of the passionate interest they take in their themes. They give us the very heart of a man on every page. Writing is to them the same thing as living. It is articulate living. Now, curiously enough, Shakespeare belongs to this class of writers. While using a most abstract and impersonal vehicle, he became early in life so interested in his themes that his personal mind was absorbed into his work, and his personal experiences and reflections were at the disposal of his artistic requirements. The vehicle which he used is ostensibly an abstract vehicle, perhaps the most abstract literary form that exists; for the author of a play has apparently no

SHAKESPEARE

voice at all. And yet Shakespeare expressed
his most intimate personal experiences with
such fluency that you might say his vehicle
rules him. As the man in the street rumi-
nates and is greatly at the mercy of accident
for the turn in his thought, so Shakespeare.
His theme runs away with him in the good
plays, and refuses to run away with him in
the bad plays. He has so many different
planes of brilliancy that he can "pull off," as
they say, almost anything; but he is never
aiming at anything in particular when he
begins. For instance, in the *Taming of the
Shrew* he has on the background of his canvas a superficial old Italian comedy of manners and of horse-play. He botches a
boisterous, amusing and not beautiful play
out of it. How coarse is his brush here!
The subject has amused him and excited his
wit; but first-rate comedy cannot be made
out of this material,—at least, so it seems.
In *Romeo and Juliet,* Shakespeare's enormous romanticism is excited, as it is in *Antony and Cleopatra.* The subject enchants
him. There is a dream quality in all he
writes here which is at the bottom of the
popularity of these plays. But he is still at
the mercy of his dream. In *Julius Cæsar*
the interest of the play fails after the assas-

[ 167 ]

sination; the drama breaks in two. Why did not Shakespeare use the assassination as a climax, and so save this play? Because his old training in chronicle-plays suggested another course. When Shakespeare sits down to write a play about Julius Cæsar, he seizes North's *Plutarch* in his left hand and begins to write immediately. He is not thinking of how to make a drama. He is thinking about the man Cæsar and his history. And some French writer, whose name I forget, has said that the few words spoken by Cæsar in this play give the best picture of Cæsar that exists. In *Winter's Tale* the whole action is broken in two by one of those twenty-years-after, dismal arrangements which are so hard to listen to; but Shakespeare's own romantic feeling saves the play. It is saved by Shakespeare's personal charm, by his love of Perdita and of the pastoral scenes, by his passionate sentiment for Hermione and the reconciliation, by his enjoyment of Paulina and the baby. What Shakespeare does is always makeshift,—or rather inspiration. Thus, *Winter's Tale,* which begins coldly and in one of his worst manners, turns, through the turn of the plot, and quite unconsciously to the poet, into a fervent palinode in praise of conjugal love. It is shot through with personal emotion, and drips with the dews of dawn. Some people can hardly bear the excessive sentiment of *Winter's Tale;* and I confess that the reconveyance of Hermione to the breast of Leontes taxes my powers of consumption. But Shakespeare himself revelled in this. Shakespeare had, indeed, a school-girl side, the side that delights in keepsakes, in twin cherries, in long-treasured, innocent, early, passionate thoughts of happiness. The intensity of his feeling increases with the innocence of the matter in hand. This virginity of feeling, which gave us Cordelia and Desdemona, Ophelia and Miranda, governs the climax of *Winter's Tale.*

It has become customary to say that we know nothing of Shakespeare the man. But indeed we know his mind more intimately than we know the mind of any other historic person. The man himself we know : it is his method that defies our comprehension. His method is not an intellectual thing at all, and has never been reduced to a shape in which it can be studied. His method is a part of his digestion and of his daily life. The thing he laid his hand to he transmutes. At an earlier or later period of his life, *King Lear* would have turned under his hands

into a rural comedy, or into a golden drama,
like *The Merchant of Venice.*

Power in expression arises out of artistic
unity, whether in comedy or tragedy; and in
Shakespeare's good plays the whole volume
of the drama rolls along in its own envelope,
and with a natural flow like a tide of the
ocean. Every word and metaphor, every
character and incident, is drenched in a particular tint and cloud-colour. The whole
thing is like a solid body, so unitary is its
complexity; and as it rolls it invades our
minds with the force of nature—our own
nature. The law of its behaviour suits our
mind so exactly that the fable seems to be a
part of ourselves: a child can understand it.
This can be said of Shakespeare only at his
easiest and best, for there is also a Shakespeare who lumbers and jolts about, poses,
makes bad jokes, breaks off in the middle, is
obscene and contradictory, dull and horrid.
For Shakespeare was the most careless
writer that ever lived, and it is this careless-
ness which left him so open to the whisper-
ings of the Muse.

Even the bad plays have individuality;
each has a psychological character of its
own; they do not resemble one another in
spirit. And the Shakespeare who moves in

and out of the bad plays, appearing and dis-
appearing like a silent scene-shifter who is
not meant to be observed, resembles the
Shakespeare of the great plays in the length
of his stride. He is not always radiant or at
home in the play. He is often queer, sour,
and low-minded, like a sick man. We recognise his mind, however, through its preoccupation with abstract thoughts expressed in
dazzling, concrete images.

# IV

## TROILUS AND CRESSIDA

THERE is a history of criticism which will go on forever, and Shakespeare's relation to it is indubitably very important. But Shakespeare's direct influence upon the great body of men who know nothing about this whole branch of learning is what makes him Shakespeare. The Gospels are not encrusted in theology, because biblical criticism has never adhered to the New Testament. So literary and dramatic criticism do not stick to Shakespeare. There is some sort of *vis major* behind the Gospels, and there is a *vis major* behind much of Shakespeare which nothing touches. This power draws and fascinates the scholar; it chains him to his desk and to his thesis; it does not, as a rule, liberate his intellect. The scholar whose imagination is alive is a rarity. Indeed, scholarship proverbially kills the imagination; and therefore in striving to find what is our own in Shakespeare—who is the greatest storehouse of imagination in the world—we should be indifferent to scholarship. Everyone of us has a personal share in this wealth, a special relation to this mountainous loadstone of attracting intellect. No matter what we find, we cannot carry it away, nor can we ever force anyone else to perceive and value our discovery exactly as we do.

Coleridge discovered two different Shakespeares in *All's Well that Ends Well*. This is the right spirit in which to read Shakespeare,—this free-handed plundering of his meanings. We should read Shakespeare for pleasure, and only for pleasure. The plays were meant to be gay trifles, the perfume and the suppliance of a minute. Music and painting and poetry yield up their meanings in flashes and by accident; and just here is where the critics go mad: for they think to bore into the meaning of poetry as a mouse bores into a cheese. A man who sits down to read *The Tempest* for six months at a stretch is sure to make some discovery about the play. The professional scholars who attack ancient poetry and lost religions in this spirit of conquest are always rewarded: they find something. They develop a hobby, a thesis, an *idée fixe*. They become inter-

ested in a discovery of some sort; and the
life of the subject closes its portals.

So, then, let us be unscholarly, careless,
and above all let us take no stock in our own
discoveries, but regard the world as Dream
Stuff, while we examine the extremely unpleasant play of *Troilus and Cressida,*—a
play that can never have been good; for it
has no humour, no dramatic force, no sustained beauty. It has neither action nor
plot, neither wit nor intention; and it is per-
vaded by a low moral tone. It is, indeed, a
horrid jumble of distasteful impressions.
And yet the play is intimately and con-
vincingly Shakespeare's own. My reason
for taking it up is that we seem to find in it
broken bits of Shakespeare's art, botches and
scraps of him, often so crudely done as to
lay bare the artist's intention without accom-
plishing his end. By studying these stray
passages we seem to get some insight into
the way the poet's mind worked.

*Troilus and Cressida* is supposed to concern the Trojan War; but no war seems to
be in progress in it. Certain characters, or
caricatures, wander on and off the stage, or
offend us by their different breaches of taste.
The dressing up of the Homeric heroes in
Elizabethan costume produces burlesque.

## GREEK GENIUS

The principal characters suggest the oper-
etta, and the minor ones the music-hall.
Ajax appears as a sort of Bardolph or
Pistol; Pandarus as an Andrew Aguecheek;
Thersites as a Shakespearian clown—*e.g.*,
Launcelot Gobbo, Autolycus. Helen is addressed by Paris as "Nell." Ulysses walks
upon the stage reading a letter. Hector, in
speaking to Menelaus, refers to Helen as
"your quondam wife," to which Menelaus
replies, "Name her not now, sir; she's a
deadly theme." "O pardon, I offend," says
Hector. We find it hard to credit Shakespeare with the worst parts of the dialogue;
but the man who adopted and republished
the lines is almost as much a reprobate as the
man who wrote them.

There are many speeches in the play that
no one but Shakespeare could have written,
—not a juvenile Shakespeare, either, but the
Shakespeare of *King Lear* and *Macbeth,* the
full-grown, miracle-minded man. These
good things detach themselves like new paint
from an old canvas; but the canvas is covered with truly Shakespearian work,—only
bad, unpleasant work,—so that some scholars have supposed that *Troilus and Cressida*
was a youthful piece worked over by the
mature artist. Whether the play be old or

[ 176 ]

new, and whether the kernel of it be Shakespeare's own or another's, we can observe in it the working of Shakespeare's intelligence. Not only is the awakened great genius there, but the deboshed penny-a-liner is there also, all through the play. Besides these two men there is, here and there, a half-awakened Shakespeare, a boozy, indifferent Orpheus, who gropes past his thought and lunges on, sometimes swinging out a phrase like a wreath of roses and then again heaving a brick. All the beauties in the play are detached and scrappy things. That Shakespeare took no coherent interest in the story whenever he wrote it, or wrote *at* it,—of this we feel sure.

The play opens with a couple of scenes in the pot-house vein between Pandarus, Troilus, and Cressida; and then the Grecian leaders come on with a few long speeches in Shakespeare's most magnificent rhetoric, larded with his most personal and peculiar faults. Indeed, in this play most of his bold misuses of language are *infelicitous*. But the wreaths of roses are there also. As to the meaning of the play, we should gather from the long opening speeches that the plot was to have something to do with the perils

of a divided authority; for this idea is given
out by Agamemnon and then expanded and
worked up by Ulysses in two speeches, of
which the first is didactic and stately, somewhat like Portia's on the quality of mercy,
and the second is a description, in a vein to
make Homer weep, of the buffoonery practised in the tent of Achilles.  The perils of a
divided authority provide a philosophic
theme on which the profound psychologist
Shakespeare has reflected much, and the
poetry comes boiling out of him as from a
spring.  Then it stops.

Thersites, the most degraded and most
monstrous of Shakespeare's clowns, is now
given his whack at the audience, and Ajax
is presented as the stupid man.  Then follows a family scene between Hector, Troilus,
and Priam, in which the merits of the war
are discussed.  Hector happens to remark
of Helen: "She is not worth what she doth
cost the holding."  This awakens, or half
awakens, the sleeping philosopher in Shakespeare, and he gropes in his dream for his
favourite thought: "There's nothing good
or bad but thinking makes it so."  This
thought always swims in deep waters; it is a
most difficult thought to express, as the

# SHAKESPEARE

Pragmatists have recently found; and Shakespeare's delivery of it upon the present occasion is so clumsy that we hardly know where he stands on the argument.

*Troilus.* What is aught but as 'tis valued?
*Hector.* But value dwells not in particular
    will;
  It holds his estimate and dignity
  As well wherein 'tis precious of itself
  As in the prizer. 'Tis mad idolatry
  To make the service greater than the god,
  And the will dotes that is inclinable
  To what infectiously itself affects,
  Without some image of the affected merit.

Here, as so often in Shakespeare, everything both on and off the stage is held up while the master talks to himself in his own half-intelligible lingo about the secret problems of his thought. There must somewhere exist, thinks Shakespeare, a reality of which our thought is the image. A very similar passage occurs when Troilus discovers the perfidy of Cressida and proceeds to reason in an uninspired way about abstractions. His Cressida could not act thus; then there must be two Cressidas:

[179]

*Troilus.* . . . O madness of discourse,
That cause sets up with and against thyself!
Bi-fold authority! where reason can re-
   volt
Without perdition, and loss assume all
   reason.


It may be remarked that all through
Shakespeare we come upon passages which
we must read twice, because we must find
the key to them; and the key is generally
something profound. A page or two earlier
in this play Cressida says: "Blind fear
that, seeing reason leads, finds safer footing
than blind reason stumbling without fear.
To fear the worst oft cures the worst." His
mind is so full of these abstractions that he
tumbles them out sometimes in paradox.
In moments of great excitement he makes
them sing. But in *Troilus and Cressida*
there is nothing to stimulate him to the pitch
where philosophy turns into music.
   On the other hand, those easier thoughts
and more familiar themes which are the
give-and-take of drama live so within his
mastery that any pebble sets them off, as,
for instance, the thought of *honour*. At the

# SHAKESPEARE

close of the family scene Troilus speaks with
the tongue of Henry V:

*Troilus.*  Why, there you touched the life of
        our design:
   Were it not glory that we more affected
   Than the performance of our heaving
        spleens,
   I would not wish a drop of Trojan blood
   Spent more in her defence.  But, worthy
        Hector,
   She is a theme of honour and renown,
   A spur to valiant and magnanimous
        deeds,
   Whose present courage may beat down
        our foes,
   And fame, in time to come, canonise us:
   For, I presume, brave Hector would not
        lose
   So rich advantage of a promis'd glory
   As smiles upon the forehead of this
        action
   For the wide world's revenue.

Immediately upon this fluent and appro-
priate climax there follows more Thersites,
and a scene in which Ajax is made the butt
of sham flattery,—all most truly Shakespearian and most truly horse-play.

[ 181 ]

GREEK GENIUS

We now approach the great scene of the play, in which Ulysses endeavours to persuade Achilles to abandon his ill-humour and fight. It seems impossible that Shakespeare should have read any translation of Homer, though he is supposed to have read Chapman; for Shakespeare imagines that Achilles' wrath was the result of sheer, motiveless ill-temper. He neglects the splendid dramatic reason for the wrath, namely, that the girl Briseis had been reft from Achilles by Agamemnon. Ulysses, then, after gaining the attention of Achilles by a ruse, approaches him with an argument based upon a philosophic abstraction so intellectual that Plato would have pricked up his ears at it. But no one except a professional casuist would be apt to guess what Ulysses was talking about:

*Ulysses.*　　　A strange fellow here
　Writes me: That man, how dearly ever
　　　parted,
　How much in having, or without or in,
　Cannot make boast to have that which he
　　　hath,
　Nor feels not what he owes, but by
　　　reflection;

[ 182 ]

# SHAKESPEARE

As when his virtues shining upon others
Heat them, and they retort that heat again
To the first giver.

Achilles' reply surprises us, because it is
academic, lacking all heat and passion. He
thinks Ulysses' idea is very suggestive, very
helpful.

*Achilles.*     This is not strange, Ulysses.
  The beauty that is borne here in the face
  The bearer knows not, but commends
      itself
  To others' eyes: nor doth the eye itself,
  That most pure spirit of sense, behold
      itself,
  Not going from itself; but eye to eye
      oppos'd
  Salutes each other with each other's form:
  For speculation turns not to itself
  Till it hath travell'd, and is married there
  Where it may see itself. This is not
      strange at all.

Ulysses "distinguishes," as the logicians
would say:

*Ulysses.* I do not strain at the position,
  It is familiar, but at the author's drift. . . .

# GREEK GENIUS

Ulysses now develops his proposition, which is that men receive their own spiritual fulfilment through the effect which they produce upon others. The thought here reaches its last attenuation. The two heroes seem to be absorbed in bending over a game of metaphysical checkers. Then Ulysses launches his great, beautiful exhortation, one of the most remarkable speeches in all Shakespeare:

*Ulysses.*  Time hath, my lord, a wallet at
      his back,
  Wherein he puts alms for oblivion;
  A great-siz'd monster of ingratitudes:
  Those scraps are good deeds past; which
      are devour'd
  As fast as they are made, forgot as soon
  As done: perseverance, dear my lord,
  Keeps honour bright: to have done, is to
      hang
  Quite out of fashion, like a rusty mail
  In monumental mockery.  Take the
      instant way;
  For honour travels in a strait so narrow,
  Where one but goes abreast: keep then
      the path;
  For emulation hath a thousand sons
  That one by one pursue: if you give way,

# SHAKESPEARE

Or hedge aside from the direct forthright,
Like to an enter'd tide, they all rush by,
And leave you hindmost;
Or, like a gallant horse fall'n in first rank,
Lie there for pavement to the abject rear,
O'errun and trampled on: then what they
    do in present,
Though less than yours in past, must
    o'ertop yours;
For time is like a fashionable host
That slightly shakes his parting guest by
    the hand,
And with his arms outstretch'd, as he
    would fly,
Grasps-in the comer: welcome ever smiles,
And farewell goes out sighing.  O, let not
    virtue seek
Remuneration for the thing it was;
For beauty, wit,
High birth, vigour of bone, desert in
    service,
Love, friendship, charity, are subjects all
To envious and calumniating time.
One touch of nature makes the whole
    world kin,
That all with one consent praise new-born
    gawds,
Though they are made and moulded of
    things past,

## GREEK GENIUS

And give to dust that is a little gilt
More laud than gilt o'er-dusted.
The present eye praises the present object:
Then marvel not, thou great and complete
    man,
That all the Greeks begin to worship
    Ajax;
Since things in motion sooner catch the
    eye
Than what not stirs.  The cry went once
    on thee,
And still it might, and yet it may again,
If thou wouldst not entomb thyself alive,
And case thy reputation in thy tent;
Whose glorious deeds, but in these fields
    of late,
Made emulous missions 'mongst the gods
    themselves,
And drave great Mars to faction.

The head and flow of eloquence in this
speech carries Shakespeare over into a senseless but magnificent eulogy of the secret service of Agamemnon's government, through
whose clever work Achilles' attachment to
one of Priam's daughters has been discovered.  The eloquence is checked suddenly,
however, by a ditch of bad taste, almost of
obscenity, and ends in a few flat lines.  Such

[ 186 ]

## SHAKESPEARE

is Shakespeare,—so unconscious, so indifferent; so at the mercy of what is in progress
before him and within him; so unprincipled
in his art; so gifted in his mind.

There is yet another page of the play on
which shines a genius like that of *Romeo
and Juliet*. Something in the sudden and
enforced parting of Troilus and Cressida
reminds Shakespeare of the tender agony of
such partings, which he must himself have
known or he could not have written:

*Troilus.*  .  .  .  .  .

   We two, that with so many thousand
      sighs
   Did buy each other, must poorly sell
      ourselves
   With the rude brevity and discharge of
      one.
   Injurious time now with a robber's haste
   Crams his rich thievery up, he knows not
      how:
   As many farewells as be stars in heaven,
   With distinct breath and consign'd kisses
      to them,
   He fumbles up into a loose adieu:
   And scants us with a single famish'd kiss,
   Distasted with the salt of broken tears.

GREEK GENIUS

I have not cited the little golden bits that gleam through *Troilus and Cressida*. Any reader can find them for himself. But there is no foil of drama behind these stray jewels. The play constantly reminds us of Shakespeare's other worlds. Perhaps it supplied him with no controlling mood, and he was thus led to filch from his other moods. One might think that the following lines must come out of *Othello*. Troilus is warning Cressida not to forget him among the dances and gaieties of the Grecian camp:

. . . . . .

But I can tell that in each grace of these
There lurks a still and dumb-discoursive
    devil
That tempts most cunningly. But be not
    tempted.

I must cite also a clever remark about women which is put in the mouth of Ulysses by the great observer and lover of women, Shakespeare. It is coldly and somewhat coarsely said, and is extremely abstract, intellectual, world-wise; yet it records and pictures a certain type of woman very perfectly:

[ 188 ]

# SHAKESPEARE

*Ulysses.* . . . . . .

O! these encounterers, so glib of tongue,
That give accosting welcome ere it comes,
And wide unclasp the tables of their
    thoughts
To every ticklish reader, set them down
For sluttish spoils of opportunity,
And daughters of the game.

Throughout the play we have been in contact with the power of abstract reasoning, clothed at times in images so bright and easy as to make it beautiful, fading at times into commonplace, and often replaced by feeble humour and empty talk. The fact that the theme does not interest the poet isolates the jets of his talent and in some degree analyses the man for us. There is, as it were, no character-interest in this play, no Iago, no Shylock, no Romeo; and there is no plot. I can find no unity in it, and yet it is full of the greatest talent for writing that a man ever possessed. This talent seems to roll about like a hulk in the trough of the sea.

But Shakespeare knew nothing of all this. He was as much at home in the mud as in the rainbow, and spent perhaps not so much time over his *Troilus and Cressida* as any one will who tries to understand the play. Shakespeare had no intentions, but wrote as Mozart wrote. Very unlike Mozart was he: for parts of Shakespeare are ugly, and much of him is whimsical, and some of him is perverted. But his work is all a natural product, like the silk-worm's thread. One can never be quite sure that even Thersites may not show under the microscope some beautiful pattern on his back, as Caliban does.

Perhaps half the error in the world results from providing other people with intentions; and perhaps the unique power of Shakespeare consists in the fact that he had none. He rolls in the waters of his thought, fathoms deep, without attempt to save himself, without interest or knowledge as to where he is or in what direction he moves. He is unconscious, like an infant; and opening his eyes on the nearest object, remembers the remotest with no consciousness of transition. His mind is like a windmill that makes no effort, but merely transmits natural force; and his thoughts hit us with the power of all nature behind them. They are ingenuous, spontaneous, almost unexamined.

# V

## THE MELANCHOLY PLAYS

IN the full tide of one of Shakespeare's great arguments, as in *Lear* or in *Hamlet,* the forces are stupendous, yet through the perfection of the invisible machinery of the play there is nothing which we can take hold of, saying, "Here lies the power." It is the same with all other very great works of art. They teach us, *themselves,* but will not answer questions as to how it is done. Thus it comes about that one can best study the minds of great artists in their lesser and imperfect works. Here we find problems not too complex and a velocity of thought not so high as to defy pursuit. It is for this reason that a chapter has been devoted to *Troilus and Cressida;* and for the same reason it is well to turn over the leaves of Shakespeare's other minor plays by the light of whatever we happen to know, whether of life or of literature.

Shakespeare was subject to fits of gloomy

depression, or he never could have left behind such sad documents as some of these
minor plays. How far the melancholy is
due to the plot, and how far to the poet's
own circumstances, we can never know.
But we may assume that Shakespeare's
mood as we find it in any play was the mood
which governed him in the choice of the
story. *All's Well that Ends Well* falls into
the list of plays that leave us sad. Melancholy moulders in the very title of it; for
we feel that all is not well nor ever has been
nor can be well again. There was not much
in the box of life; and there has been a great
pother about opening it and shutting it, and
at last it is shut up with a triumphant and
sudden major chord, but the box is empty.
*All's Well that Ends Well* is one of the plays
in which an Italian plot proves to be an indigestible morsel to the English playwright.
Why could not Shakespeare have treated
this plot in the spirit of the *Taming of the
Shrew,* which makes no moral appeal? The
reason is that behind Shakespeare's *Taming
of the Shrew* there was an old Italian comedy which gave him his colouring, whereas
in *All's Well* he is adapting an older English
play, which had taken an Italian fable seriously. The plot is at war with the drama-

tist, and neither one comes off wholly victorious. In some of his Italian stories— as in *Romeo and Juliet*—Shakespeare transmutes all the characters into himself, and triumphs. But in others he fails. The tales of the Italian prelate Bandello, in which wives disguise themselves and seduce their husbands, soldiers stab and throw dice, widows climb in and out of windows, and all men wear masks and take life lightly, are so foreign to Northern sentiment, that in giving them life Shakespeare often equivocates. The plot of *All's Well* is as follows: A maid cures a sick king, who promises to give her whatever bridegroom she shall choose in marriage. She chooses Bertram, with whom she has long been in love, and who flees the court upon the announcement that he must wed her. The rest of the story consists in the lady's contriving a secret assignation with Bertram, unknown to the man himself, who thereupon repents, marries her, and "all's well." Such a degraded plot might well daunt a romantic spirit. Even the genius of Shakespeare has been foiled by this material. There is no character in *All's Well that Ends Well* that can attract us, except the old Countess Mother, who is a secondary subject, a still-life portrait, and

Lafeu, the old lord, who is a happy thought, done with a few strokes by the great playwright. The other characters are rendered gloomy by the exigencies of the plot. Bertram has been carefully understood, from the Northern point of view, as a sneak; Helena is sentimentalised in a manner so at war with her conduct as to make her repellent; Parolles is a bore.

There are points in this play, as in all the others, in which Shakespeare never fails. You may call him up at one in the morning, after he has left the tavern at midnight, and he will give you the speech of the innocent young girl at any desired length and of unfailing beauty. So, in this play, the speeches of the heroine, Helena, at the beginning of the play are charming,—till we find out what her course of action is to be. She starts off, as it were, with being Miranda; but, having cured the King, she bargains for a husband as follows:

*Helena.*  Then shalt thou give me with thy kingly hand
What husband in thy power I will command:
Exempted be from me the arrogance

[ 194 ]

# SHAKESPEARE

To choose from forth the royal blood of
    France,
My low and humble name to propagate
With any branch or image of thy state;
But such a one, thy vassal, whom I know
Is free for me to ask, thee to bestow.

Miranda soon disappears in the Italian intrigue, and never comes out alive. In the
end Helena plays the part of a bawd. Perhaps this plot might have been carried
through as a fairy story; but Shakespeare
treats it with naturalism. He is doing his
best with the tale, and grinds away at Parolles and at the episode of the drum. Why
is not all this genial and amusing, like Falstaff or *Twelfth Night?* Shakespeare's
heart is not in it, nor his head, either. There
is, in truth, nothing here to excite him. He
is conscientiously and cleverly staging the
story, which is artificial and mundane.
There is no point at which he can deliver a
metaphysical remark about the other world.
—Yes, there is one; and the words are put
into the mouth of Lafeu, who comments
upon the King's recovery as follows:

"They say miracles are past; and we have
our philosophical persons, to make modern

and familiar things supernatural and cause-
less. Hence is it that we make trifles of terrors, ensconcing ourselves into seeming
knowledge, when we should submit ourselves
to an unknown fear."

The profundity of Lafeu's idea is aston-
ishing, and amounts to this: every explanation of the miraculous is superficial; behind
all there must be a deeper miracle, which is
not explained. The King's recovery reminds Shakespeare of this whole field of
thought; but the action of the play presses,
and he moves on.

At the bottom of our distress over Helena
in *All's Well* there lies a dramatic difficulty.
What we call a character in a play is a result,
and not a prefigured idea. Shakespeare's
characters result from his plots; and where
a story is too artificial, even Shakespeare
can do no more than throw out occasionally
a good idea which is neutralised by the
sequel. No matter how great a painter may
be, he cannot admit false lights into his canvas without spoiling its atmosphere. In
romantic drama a character is a mere drawing in smoke,—perfect so long as it is un-
touched, but the merest breath will confuse
it. Cordelia lives in her few speeches, and is

as solid as marble. If the plot of *King Lear* had required some subsequent banality from Cordelia, Shakespeare would not have hesitated for a moment. He would have dashed it in and gone to dinner, and we of the twentieth century should have been made to feel a little gloomy by it.

In *Measure for Measure* there is a much severer gloom than in *All's Well*. Here is a comedy to make a man drown himself and have Shakespeare's name carved on his tomb. There is a running accompaniment of great intellect in this play, whose action goes forward in a twilight of blighted silver, with no sunlight in it. In the poetic scenes there is the rhetoric of Prospero without his power. In the comic interludes there is the manner of Eastcheap without its humour.

Here again, as in *All's Well*, the innocent woman receives the few streaming shafts from heaven in a couple of scenes of great tragedy. The rest of the play follows out in detail a painful intrigue, through which the villain, Angelo, is safely married off to his old neglected sweetheart, Mariana of the Moated Grange. In the somewhat sudden wind up, every one shakes hands all round in a fashion worthy of Dickens, and the curtain falls.

## GREEK GENIUS

In *Measure for Measure* the suggestion
of the wicked Judge, Angelo, that he shall
pardon Isabella's brother, but at the price of
her own honour, gives rise to a tragic situation of the first magnitude; and the play
immediately soars into tragedy as naturally
as if *Lear* were on the stage. Isabella is a
novice in a convent. Her directness and
promptitude of mind are as marked as
her innocence. Shakespeare's good women
never understand evil. When her brother's
friend, Lucio, the man about town, explains
to her that her brother, Claudio, has been
condemned to death through the enforce-
ment of the old law against adultery, she
does not comprehend. Her innocence strikes
poetry into the debauchee. He apologises
for his plainness of speech:

*Lucio.* . . . . . . .
   I hold you as a thing ensky'd, and sainted
   By your announcement, an immortal
       spirit,
   And to be talk'd with in sincerity,
   As with a saint.

He explains the matter again, and in language which no one can mistake. She
understands now, but is not sure.

SHAKESPEARE

*Isabella.* Someone with child by him?—My
cousin Juliet?

It is agreed that she shall intercede
with the Judge, Angelo. At her second
interview with Angelo, when he proposes
the infamous bargain, she misunderstands
for a long time, and then bursts into flame
as naturally as a peasant woman might do:

*Ang.* Believe me, on mine honour,
My words express my purpose.
*Isab.* Ha! little honour to be much believed,
And most pernicious purpose!—Seeming,
seeming!—
I will proclaim thee, Angelo; look for 't:
Sign me a present pardon for my brother,
Or with an outstretched throat I'll tell the
world
Aloud what man thou art.

It next becomes her duty to consult
Claudio, her brother, about the whole matter. And Claudio is shaken by the fear of
death. This is one of Shakespeare's besieg-
ing thoughts, and the young Claudio, a
somewhat unideaed youth, speaks with the
tongue of Hamlet's father:

[ 199 ]

# GREEK GENIUS

Ay, but to die, and go we know not
    where;
To lie in cold obstruction, and to rot;
This sensible warm motion to become
A kneaded clod; and the delighted spirit
To bathe in fiery floods, or to reside
In thrilling regions of thick-ribbed ice;
To be imprison'd in the viewless winds,
And blown with restless violence round
    about
The pendant world; or to be worse than
    worst
Of those that lawless and incertain
    thoughts
Imagine howling!—'tis too horrible.
The weariest and most loathed worldly
    life,
That age, ache, penury, and imprisonment
Can lay on nature is a paradise
To what we fear of death.
*Isab.*   Alas! alas!
*Claud.*        Sweet sister, let me live.
What sin you do to save a brother's life,
Nature dispenses with the deed so far
That it becomes a virtue.
*Isab.*         O you beast!
O faithless coward! O dishonest wretch!
Wilt thou be made a man out of my vice?
Is 't not a kind of incest, to take life

From thine own sister's shame?  What
    should I think?
Heaven shield, my mother play'd my
    father fair;
For such a warped slip of wilderness
Ne'er issu'd from his blood.  Take my
    defiance:
Die; perish!  Might but my bending down
Reprieve thee from thy fate, it should
    proceed.
I'll pray a thousand prayers for thy death,
No word to save thee.

Here is womanhood from queen to peasant, and drama from eternity to eternity.
But there is not much of either in *Measure
for Measure,*—not enough of either to drag
the play in the great procession of Shakespeare's tragedies.  For this same woman,
Isabella, at the close of the play is made to
simulate another woman in making (not
keeping) an assignation.  The innocent,
fiery Isabella of the earlier act would never
have consented to play out the licentious
Italian comedy which Shakespeare casts her
for in the last act.  The spectator feels this,
and resents the soil which Shakespeare has
cast on his own creation.  But for this
slander, Isabella would have taken her place

beside Desdemona and Imogen. But Shakespeare sometimes had bad taste; or, rather,
he had no taste at all: for taste is conscious
art.

While all these things have been going on
in *Measure for Measure,* the rightful Duke
has made a pretended abdication, and has
been moving about in the disguise of a friar,
ready to appear as *deus ex machina* at the
proper moment. For some reason which I
cannot fathom this device is dramatically
ineffective. It would have been better if the
old Duke had been kept entirely out of the
way till the climax. But in that case we
should have missed another most Shakespearian lecture on death which the Duke-as-
Friar delivers in the jail to the condemned
Claudio, and which colours the play.

*Claud.* The miserable have no other
        medicine,
    But only hope.
    I have hope to live, and am prepar'd to
        die.
*Duke.* Be absolute for death; either death,
        or life,
    Shall thereby be the sweeter. Reason thus
        with life:—
    If I do lose thee, I do lose a thing

SHAKESPEARE

> That none but fools would keep; a breath
>     thou art,
> Servile to all the skyey influences,
> That do this habitation, where thou
>     keep'st,
> Hourly afflict. . . .

In this long speech, of which I give only
the opening, Hamlet, Macbeth, Prospero,
Touchstone, and many others peep out, but
there is no new character.  The speech is a
gloomy and decorative bit of rhetoric, sincere only in that it somehow depicts Shakespeare's mood.  As for Angelo himself,
with his gravity, his sudden, unconvincing
lust, and his final happy marriage, the plot
precludes his being a human character at all.
There is no such man.  It must be observed,
in closing *Measure for Measure,* that the
whole play is marked by a quite unnecessary
grossness,—the indecency which goes with
melancholy and is a part of it.

Every one should read *Timon of Athens,*
and see whether a moral can be drawn out of
it.  Shakespeare seems to have chosen the
plot because he was in ill-humour, perhaps
sick.  Feeling thoroughly cynical, he seems
to have expected to write a cynical play.  The
cynicism in *Timon,* however, is so evenly

distributed among so many characters that
all the dramatic effect of it is lost. The play
is thus without idea, and its incidents are
absurdly dull. A sort of malevolence ex-
hales from it, but nothing that can be
thought of as philosophy. Timon, after a
life of senseless expenditure, grows poor,
and is surprised to find that his creditors and
the sycophants who had surrounded him in
prosperity do not love him in his disgrace.
He therefore leaves Athens and digs in the
earth for roots. In digging he finds gold,
and with this he subsidises Alcibiades, who
is also in exile, to avenge the injuries of
both by destroying Athens. The play is too
Elizabethan, too near the charade, and too
shallow to be interesting as a play; but it is
full of truly Shakespearian touches in the
language. Shakespeare's genius has evidently been unable to take hold of this material. It was his habit to seize his themes
experimentally, and he never knew what was
coming out of a plot. He began at once,
without knowing just where he was to end,
and he never found the same theme twice.
His most tremendous effects are due to this
method, and his "effects defective" also
come by this cause. When tragedy unrolls
out of his gossamer, it arrives as a gift of

SHAKESPEARE

nature,—born, not made. It has the brilliancy of the humming-bird and the edge of the sword-lily's leaf. *Romeo and Juliet* has in it the morn and liquid dew of youth. When the subject yields no tragedy, as in *Coriolanus*,—why, then you may take what you get. There was nothing in the subject, as it turns out. We can blame nobody for our disappointments in the Melancholy Plays. No one is responsible.

# VI

## SHAKESPEARE'S INFLUENCE

CONTACT with Shakespeare's large, impersonal mind makes us bigger. A man does not need to read a play through in order to receive the poet's influence, which is like an electric stimulation and affects our whole being, though we receive it through the finger-tips. If one could find two boys of twelve who were exactly alike, and if one of them should begin to read Shakespeare with interest, he would become more intelligent than the other lad within fifteen minutes. The acceptability of Shakespeare to the young is one of his divinest qualities. There is, as it were, a ready-made world which Shakespeare slides into our minds long before we are capable of receiving the real world. This Shakespearian world is healthier, happier, and infinitely cleverer than the real world. Its eloquence is running at a high speed, and the smallest contact with any word in it makes our entire system stand erect.

Shakespeare's intelligence was completely developed. There were matters that did not interest him; but everything that he knew was co-ordinated. He always speaks from the same pulpit. This is not obvious,—indeed, it is the last thing that many people would say about him,—because we do not know where that pulpit was, nor how he got into it. But his phrases always come from the same personality, from the same intellectual outlook. It is as if the human soul consisted of an infinite series of concentric spheres, one inside the other, and Shakespeare's voice always caused the same sphere to resound. When we hear the ring of it we cry, "Shakespeare!" in our sleep. He is a metaphysical unity, and all his characters are merely Shakespeare—Shakespeare with rays of humour about his head, or with an old cloak from some royal coronation upon his shoulders. We cannot distinguish between the man and the artist. The man and the artist are one.

It is this disappearance of the man into the artist, by the way, that has so puzzled the world about Shakespeare's personality. People are ever searching for the mask, and

there is no mask.  Ambition is what reveals
men, and he had no ambition.  Motive is
what shows men's contours, and he had no
motive.  He had no desire to conceal himself, but he vanishes in a witticism because
he is all wit.  During his lifetime he was so
logically perfect in his indifference that no
one especially noticed his existence; and he
passed through life as a pleasant fellow of
no great importance, leaving such a minimum
of personal reminiscences in the minds of
his contemporaries that people now think
him a mystery.  The real mystery, however,
is one which the knowledge of personal
facts could not solve for us.

He has left the most powerful record of
the kind of man he must have been by leaving
a vacuum.  His life and mind are a monument to the unknowable.  The vanishing-
point is in every moment of his thought and
in every line of his work, and he has van-
ished into it.  The average man is puzzled
by this outcome.  He thinks that the infinite
is an algebraical term or a poetic sentiment;
and Shakespeare presents him with the infinite in flesh and blood.

There are certain very categorical minds,
often very strong minds, that feel a chal-
lenge in this whole phenomenon of Shake-

speare's unknowability. They are excited and almost angered by it. They must and will understand. Hence the prodigious literature of quack discovery about Shakespeare. Now the quack is a man whose sentiment is not satisfied unless he discovers something that is not there. If he should find a true thing, it would coalesce with the rest of truth and somewhat defeat his ambition; he would never be satisfied with it. Each one of the new pundits has therefore a theory of his own and betrays a kind of megalomania in regard to it. All this false learning is a by-product of Shakespeare's metaphysical influence, much as the ten thousand dogmas of Christianity are the result of Christ's thought as it acts upon minds which resent the abstraction of that thought.

Shakespeare belongs to the Renaissance. We feel this quite distinctly in considering his relation to religion. Like the great pagan painters of the Italian Renaissance, he knows only so much of religion as his art teaches him,—as his art made necessary. There are some kinds of painting which imply religion. Paul Veronese, through sheer æsthetic necessity, paints a saint, paints a Pentecost. Guido Reni paints a Crucifixion which touches the sphere of religious truth. In such cases the artistic illumination suffices for the artistic need; but one step beyond it the artist does not go. So in Shakespeare there are decorative phrases of a religious beauty which is lent to him by the thing in hand,—I mean by the spiritual *mise en scène.*

For instance:

"In those holy fields
Over whose acres walked those blessed feet,
Which fourteen hundred years ago were
      nailed
For our advantage on the bitter cross."

Again:

"He gave his honours to the world again,
His blessed past to heaven, and slept in
      peace."

This kind of religious feeling in Shakespeare is a sort of feudal tapestry with which he adorns his banqueting-hall. Perhaps the political conditions of his day helped to banish religious motives from his stage. One suspects in him also an instinctive avoidance of such motives on grounds of personal feeling. At any rate, the absence

of religious motive colours the plays and
gives them their quality.

Shakespeare uses religious metaphors in
much the same way that he uses mythology;
indeed, I should say that the pagan symbolism was dearer to him than the Christian.
His whole work is tinged with the atmosphere of an imaginary antiquity, which
comes to him from translations of Ovid,
Plutarch, and Virgil, and which bears the
same relation to classic feeling that the back-
grounds in quattrocentist pictures bear to
ancient Rome. He never came near enough
to the Latin writers to be influenced by them
in style or purpose.

It is worth while to read the modest essay
entitled *Life of Shakespeare* by Nicholas
Rowe, Shakespeare's first editor, which was
published in 1709, and which, on the whole,
gives almost as good an account of the poet
as the later critics have been able to work
out. Rowe preserves a tradition, which the
English scholars have somewhat neglected,
that Shakespeare "died a Papist." That the
poet should have accepted the final ministra-
tions of a priest seems to chime in with what
one finds in the plays. The tradition accords
with the decorative piety of Shakespeare's
spirit, and with the only doctrinal prejudice

which we can certainly perceive in his work,
—namely, his dislike of the Puritans. He
could hardly have been a "good" Catholic, or
we should have found it out in a hundred
ways; but he was a romantic sceptic with a
fondness for the dramatic beauties of the old
religion. His Ghost in *Hamlet* is purgatorial
and doctrinal,—just enough so for stage
purposes. His marriages in the *Comedy of
Errors* and in *Romeo and Juliet* are—well,
they are really pagan, with a few candles and
a vague Mother Church from No-Man's-
Land standing behind. So also his burials
are scenic. The dirge over Imogen, on the
other hand, is pantheistic. This is his own
sort of religion,—and a sweet rhapsody it
is. So in most of his discourses on death the
romanticism and the scepticism reveal to us
Shakespeare's personal church.

With Shakespeare died the Renaissance
in England. The psalm-singing weavers of
whom he makes fun,—and not good-natured
fun, either,—were to rule the land within a
few years after his death. That they should
cut so little figure in these plays, which teem
with the national life, does not prove the
non-existence of the pious weavers, but only
that Shakespeare's thought did not receive
them. It shows how special and peculiar is

the world in which lives the artist,—even
the greatest artist. Every artist is an *impe-
rium in imperio,* a cathedral with perhaps a
dead town at its feet, or, as in this case, a
Renaissance palace with a live town at its
feet.

With regard to the miraculous nature of
life, Shakespeare never forgets it: it is everywhere. He resents the mere notion of
rationalism. He will not have it that any
explanation is true. Throughout *Hamlet*
and *The Tempest*—indeed, in all his plays
—he shows his acquaintance with hypno-
tism, telepathy, and the power of prayer,—
with the potency of unseen forces which rule
the world. "Spirits are not finely touched
save to fine issues." The thing in hand is a
part of something else; men are projections
of other powers, and what we see is due to
the operation of something behind. His
moralising largely consists in drawing our
attention to these phenomena. "Canst thou
who dost command the beggar's knee command the health of it?" All these manifes-
tations of spirit he knows not as theories or
beliefs. He knows them in the raw, and sees
them freshly as he speaks.

It is just because Shakespeare insists on
leaving matters in the mist in which they are

born that his thought endures. Persons who schematise the Unknowable codify themselves, and pass by with the age they live in. The crucible of Shakespeare turns all to vapour, and leaves a Shakespearian cosmos which is at every point true to itself. He thus gives us an instantaneous vision of a single one of the infinite concentric worlds that slumber in each of us.

Shakespeare's Universe is so at one with itself that it controls our attention like Greek art; and it is almost as far from the world of religion as Greek art is. That consciousness of the presence of God which invades men's emotions and almost extinguishes the visible world for them is not in Shakespeare. Moreover, that desire to communicate and spread the consciousness of God to others, which accompanies the experience, is very far from Shakespeare. It would be distasteful to him. He is with the primal intellect in such matters; and those views which are brought back and redelivered to the intellect only after the intellect has suffered a thorough plunge, and has been for a time drowned in religious emotion, are unknown to him.

I confess that the intellect often comes back melted and distorted from the drown-

ing experiences of religion, and that religion
has thus sent down through the centuries a
track of distorted intellect, side by side with
the track of sanctity, of benevolence, and of
natural power. Nevertheless, the emotional
consciousness of God is one of the most
important factors in human history. It
moulds and changes humanity. This influence did not pass through Shakespeare, and
to transmit it is no part of his function.
Thus it appears that the profoundest experience of half mankind—to wit, religion—is
not within the range of Shakespeare's sym-
pathies; and yet he remains the greatest
dramatist of the world. How does this come
about? It comes about through the rarity
of great genius, and through the vastness of
range in human life.

We can perhaps best realise the matter by
turning to some entirely different field of
thought. We see, for instance, in Beethoven
or in Bach a talent comparable to Shakespeare's, exercised in a world quite different
from Shakespeare's world.

The great artist is, indeed, a rare person.
There have been only a handful of them in
the history of western Europe. And it is a
notable thing that these great artists, while
each one speaks from his own sphere, do not

attack one another. Shakespeare does not attack Plato; nor Bach, Shakespeare. Even Chinese mysticism looms at us from the old pictures with meanings which are native to our Western sentiment.

All forms of great art are cognate and support one another. Shakespeare is probably the strongest personal influence of a purely intellectual kind in the world. He is one of the great sages of humanity who teach something to the master-intellects of each generation. And besides this, he is by far the most popular poet in the world, and teaches metaphysics to millions who do not know they are learning, but find in him merely a fellow-being who loves and understands them.

# III
# BALZAC

## BALZAC

THERE is in France a light literature which does not bear transportation. It can be properly read and enjoyed only within sight of the Institute. The works have not enough body in them to cross the Atlantic. A book of this sort becomes pretentious if read in Fifth Avenue; all the social amenities which must be read between the lines of it drop to the bottom of the flask and become unpleasant lees. But when read in Paris, and as it comes hot from the *fauteuil,* it is charming. It is redolent of good taste and delicate sentiment; it is generally a small book, precise, well-considered and just a little (but, oh, so very little!) effete, and it flits across the Seine like a butterfly. It is really a *conférence* which has escaped through the open windows where the Academy is in session.

Such a book is Faguet's *Balzac.* This volume is one of the series of *Les Grands Écrivains Français,* which Messrs. Hachette are giving to the world, and it presents to us, in one picture, two of those figures which are peculiar to French civilisation—the Great Master Balzac and the Little Master Faguet. By a remarkable feat of draughts-manship both figures are rendered by the same line. In snipping out the silhouette of Balzac with the sharpest of little scissors, M. Faguet has left a silhouette of himself cut in the black margin that falls to the ground. We are made to feel all through the book that the things which Balzac was *not* are the things which make up M. Faguet.

This ever present sinuous line or profile divides the man of genius from his critic—separates the creative, unconscious, original mind of the artist Balzac from the sedulous mind of the critic Faguet. The men belong to different species. Balzac is a talented, lusty son of the people, who has picked up his knowledge here and there; Faguet is a careful student, who takes his college edu-cation very seriously.

Perhaps the strong points of Balzac are so well understood in France that M. Faguet feels no need of enlarging upon them. He feels justified in launching out at once upon the deficiencies of the master, upon his ig-norance, bad taste, egoism, vulgarity, clum-

# BALZAC

siness, etc. An ignorant reader would be
prone to ask: "But why does this excellent,
learned gentleman, M. Faguet, waste his
time on Balzac? The man is evidently not
worth his pains."

M. Faguet shows with a turn of his wrist
that the political principles and religious
beliefs of Balzac are not worthy to be called
ideas, and that Balzac had no *esthétique*.
Balzac lived, it appears, in a state of mental
confusion. Balzac had a low view of human
nature, and his central thought is the pes-
simism of the cynic.

But this is not all. Balzac, it appears, is
not an artist. He has no sense of proportion
and—O horror! O agony!—he *confuses
the genres;* that is to say, he mixes in disquisitions with story-telling. All of Balzac's
sins and defects are as nothing compared to
this profanation of the *genres.*

As the English reader may not understand
about the *genres,* I must quote from M.
Faguet himself. The following is but one
of many passages in which M. Faguet, with
sacred enthusiasm, protects the *genres.*

"C'est précisément la confusion des
genres. Celui qui raconte ne doit pas dis-
serter, sous peine de rendre son récit en-

nuyeux et, du reste, hybride et ambigu.
Celui qui enseigne ne doit pas *raconter* des
histoires, mais seulement apporter comme
preuves à l'appui de ce qu'il enseigne des
exemples courts, concis et ramassés, sous
peine de se faire oublier comme professeur,
comme l'autre se faisait oublier comme con-
teur.

— 'Pourquoi ne pas confondre les
genres? La distinction en est-elle aisée?' —
Parce qu'à les confondre, à les mêler, on
affaiblit l'un et on affaiblit l'autre, ce qui
fait que l'impression finale est faible."

To suggest of Balzac that "the final impression is feeble" is a novelty. This Balzac, who
is no artist, whose ideas are mere impressions which he often does not understand
himself, who mixes his *genres* so lamentably,
who has no *esthétique,* is yet the most powerful writer France ever produced, and in
influence (as Faguet confesses) must be
ranked next to Montaigne, Voltaire, and
Rousseau—this Balzac, according to M.
Faguet, writes not well, but badly. He
scarcely ever writes well, and this only when
he forgets himself. Another critic, M.
Brunetière, cited by Faguet, has been so
struck with the badness of Balzac's writing

and the badness of Molière's writing that he
has evolved a principle—*i.e.*, that it is necessary to write badly in order to represent life
("mal écrire est une condition de la repré-
sentation de la vie").  I wish that Molière
might have lived to hear this announcement,
which reminds one of his own best manner.

This whole matter of Balzac's style and
manner of writing has been dealt with by all
of his reviewers.  It is a great subject because
of Balzac's greatness.  It was treated by
Taine with a depth and originality of vision
which leave nothing to be desired.  And yet
the reader of this essay will be indulgent if
the subject comes to the surface from time
to time; for the questions raised by Balzac's
style are so intimately related to his power
that they refuse to be dismissed.  Some new
aspect of his power brings us face to face
with a new aspect of his style.

There is a charming story cited by M.
Faguet about Balzac in his prime.  At St.
Petersburg a Russian lady was talking to
him in her salon, when the door opened and
a maid-servant entered bearing a plate.
Upon hearing her mistress address the
stranger as "M. de Balzac," the maid
dropped the plate.  "This," said Balzac to
his hostess, "is fame!"

# GREEK GENIUS

Now in reading through the very clever, very precise, very academic remarks of M. Faguet, I found myself muttering: "Yes, yes; that is all very true. Balzac has no ideas, no style; his mysticism is half sham. He has no art, no education. And yet, somehow, at the back of all this there is a big dynamic force in him—behind all, through all, he clutches my heart and brain—and not mine only, but everyone's. What was it that made that servant girl drop the plate?" One could never find out this secret by reading the books of the Academy.

The function of an academy is to support good conventions, to encourage sound grammar, sensible spelling, clear handwriting. But we must not look towards academies for profound criticism. An academy always bristles with critical perceptions, but is an enemy to all genius except its own. An academy is always a sort of benevolent incubus.

There never was a nation where the standards of good taste were so sedulously maintained as they are in France; and the French Academy, which presides over these correctnesses of taste, is the visible agent of a ruling passion. The French Academy is the organised taste of a nation which loves

correctness. At first glance an observer
might conclude that the matter ended here;
and that the French Academy represented
the sum total of the national genius. A
slight acquaintance with France and with
French history would show him that quite
the reverse is true. The nation has constantly produced men who were too great to
be understood by the Academy; men by
whom—but that a law of nature forbids it—
the Academy itself would have been vitalised.

To write about Balzac is like writing
about a race or an epoch. Balzac is a literature. No one can know the whole of him,
any more than one can be acquainted with
every shop window and every alley in Paris.

If we should endeavour to cover the whole
of Balzac geographically or statistically, we
should lose the elasticity of our own minds
in the process. We should be sure to lose
Balzac himself if we made an attempt to
catch him in a drag-net.

We do not know just how his books differ
from the rest of fiction, though it is certain
that Balzac's fiction stands in a class by itself, and that it is related to human life in a
unique manner. The rest of prose fiction

came into being in order that a vehicle and a tradition might exist in which Balzac should be possible. He is the Messiah of fiction. He imposes a whole world, a romantic dispensation, an imaginary civilisation, upon the rest of humanity; and we of England or America accept this world, understand it, and live in it without abandoning our own ideals and our ways of thought. We accept it on top of our own mode of life, as an imaginative reality, as a drama of humanity—a sort of classic, as powerful as Homer, and, perhaps, as remote from ourselves as the Homeric myths are. Such is Balzac. He is a cycle of myth, and has left himself upon the earth, like a wreath of cloud, an emanation of power, which the revolutions of the globe are spreading to new lands as the years go by.

There is every sort of writing in Balzac's books, from the trivial and penny-dreadful stories of his youth to the dulness of some of the philosophic studies by which he set so much store. I am going to speak chiefly of his merits, and of these not as if I could analyse them.

Real talent is always miraculous. Anatole France makes you see the picture of an episode with such vividness that you catch your breath. You have seen it through the back of the book, and cannot find the secret of it or tell the method by which it was done though you should eat the volume as St. John ate the book in his Apocalypse. The magic of the apt word is a peculiarly French gift, and is somehow connected with the Latin world and with Latin literary tradition, and especially with the study of Horace, who outshines all his successors in the power of brevity. Horace's words are silent lightning. Now Balzac has this gift of the magical word as well as the quite opposite gift of elaborate ratiocination. He has the gift of allowing his characters to speak for themselves; the gift of talking for them; the gift of sustaining a plot as complex as Buddhist philosophy, and which moves through scenes that are brilliant and unexpected; the gift of creating an illusion of realism through the use of the most extravagant, romantic, unreal claptrap; the gift of alternately dazzling, stimulating, and informing the reader's mind till the reader gives up all hope of analysing his own sensations and surrenders himself heart and soul to the spell of the magician.

We must remember that the term "realism" which is so often applied to Balzac, and

the whole cant of criticism through which
Balzac's work is now viewed, have been invented since his day, and are ephemeral
matters. To Balzac his characters were living creatures, active forces, incarnate
ideas; and such they will remain after this
shallow and absurd talk about realism has
been forgotten.

The internal world of his fiction is the real
world for Balzac, and he contrives to make
it the real world for his readers. He does
this by methods which are so subtle that we
can rarely perceive them. Neither are the
methods intentional: they are instinctive, and
they are ever new. It is by the merest chance
that one can discover them.

He creates his effects in a thousand different ways—sometimes dramatically, sometimes logically and with painstaking effort,
sometimes through an ejaculation or an
aside of his own which seems unpremedi-
tated, intimate, and has, one would say, no
artistic right to exist. Again, he will introduce a long anecdote, holding fast to the
reader's buttonhole as he does so, and fixing
him with his eye. He thinks aloud, he
gropes; but he always lays his hand on the
truth. Under the curtain that falls on a
scene he sometimes hides a reflection of such

depth as would warrant a chapter, and he
seems not to know what he has done. Turn
the page, and he is off on a new scent: there
was no time for more. In moments of
soliloquy he often flashes in a thought having little relation to the plot, but which is
nevertheless the best thing in the book. On
other occasions he does not take the trouble
to say just what has happened at a crisis, but
leaves us to guess it from the context. The
spontaneousness of the fact passes into Balzac's way of handling it. One sees it rather
than reads of it; one experiences it rather
than sees it.

A strange fact about Balzac is that he is
always interesting; even when he bores us he
interests us. There is a residuum in his
thought. We go back to it after the book is
closed; we find it in our mind and ponder it.

He seems to be at the mercy of a whim as
to what he is going to say next. Sometimes,
in the midst of a love scene, he will give a
long discourse on the law of marriage,
dumping in a sociological treatise with a
certain parade of learning. Then, perhaps,
comes an episode which is the fulfilment of
a dramatic climax. A thousand threads
cross each other here: it is a *rond point* in
the labyrinth of the book, a place from

which one expects vistas and summaries of reflections. But no! Balzac moves on without a pause. He has, it appears, already made his effect.

His manner of procedure in writing seems to be that of a man who, having been a witness of certain events, should sit down and think aloud about them. During the process of this thinking aloud the story is told. The man does not write down all that he has seen or lived through. He sometimes omits large portions of drama, which, nevertheless, he knows all about. The events have occurred; that is enough for Balzac. The reader must pick up his information from the divagations of the witness-thinker.

All these practices are not the elaborate devices of literary art, but, on the contrary, are the habits of a man who is so very familiar with his subject that he can state it in fifty ways, and is, at best, merely giving to the reader the fringes of it. His very longest and greatest books seem to be truncated or cut down, so that the story may get itself told. He is obliged to tear out as much as he tells—so one feels—in order to finish at all.

These books are often not even divided into chapters, but move, like the Amazon

River, without a break, in one gigantic stream—overpowering, awful.

It is not only in his fiction that he excels. His letters to his sisters, to his mother, to his young nieces, to the children of Madame Hanska, are each and all the very perfection of writing. Their spontaneous, powerful, rushing, humourous gaiety is in contrast to the sombreness of his fiction and completes the man. Every line he writes is full of genius. He is the natural, inevitable writer. You cannot gag him or dam the flow of him: he writes. His mind is full of *foison*, and he is a great reaper. He harvests the crop of his thoughts.

I will give a few random examples of his methods, in order to remind the reader of their rapid quality—a sort of casual quality, which leaves us standing in the region of the unconscious, much as Rembrandt's art leaves us there. One or two of the examples shall be from *La Cousine Bette*.

Madame Hulot, a woman of fifty-five, a matron of ideal virtue, is beaten down by misfortunes until, for a moment, she loses her moral equilibrium. In a fit of despair over the misfortunes of her family she succumbs to the idea of selling her own honour to a man who has formerly made love to her, and who is the only man that, as matters stand, can save the family. This is Monsieur Crevel. Her advances are rejected with contempt. The shock saves her; and she recovers her moral poise during a long speech in which she denounces herself:

" 'Assez, monsieur Crevel!' dit madame Hulot en ne déguisant plus son dégoût et laissant paraître toute sa honte sur son visage. 'Je suis punie maintenant au delà de mon péché. Ma conscience, si violemment contenue par la main de fer de la nécessité, me crie à cette dernière insulte que de tels sacrifices sont impossibles. Je n'ai plus de fierté, je ne me courrouce point comme jadis, je ne vous dirai pas: "Sortez!" après avoir reçu ce coup mortel. J'en ai perdu le droit—je me suis offerte à vous, comme une prostituée. . . .

'Oui,' reprit-elle en répondant à un geste de dénégation, 'j'ai sali ma vie, jusqu'ici pure, par une intention ignoble; et . . . je suis sans excuse, je le savais! . . . Je mérite toutes les injures dont vous m'accablez! Que la volonté de Dieu s'accomplisse! S'il veut la mort de deux êtres dignes d'aller à lui, qu'ils meurent, je les pleurerai, je prierai pour eux! S'il veut l'humiliation de notre

## BALZAC

famille, courbons-nous sous l'épée venge-
resse, et baisons-la, chrétiens que nous
sommes! Je sais comment expier cette
honte d'un moment qui sera le tourment de
tous mes derniers jours. Ce n'est plus madame Hulot, monsieur, qui vous parle; c'est
la pauvre, l'humble pécheresse, la chrétienne
dont le cœur n'aura plus qu'un seul sentiment, le repentir, et qui sera toute à la prière
et à la charité. Je ne puis être que la dernière des femmes et la première des repenties
par la puissance de ma faute. Vous avez été
l'instrument de mon retour à la raison, à la
voix de Dieu qui maintenant parle en moi, je
vous remercie! . . .'

Elle tremblait de ce tremblement qui, depuis ce moment ne la quitta plus. Sa voix
pleine de douceur contrastait avec la fiévreuse
parole de la femme décidée au déshonneur
pour sauver une famille. Le sang aban-
donna ses joues, elle devint blanche et ses
yeux furent secs."

Crevel is touched by the beauty of Madame
Hulot's character, and words of unexpected
sympathy are exchanged between them.
Then he says:

" 'Ne tremblez plus ainsi!'

'Est-ce que je tremble?' demanda la baronne, qui ne s'apercevait pas de cette infir-
mité si rapidement venue."

Balzac has here somehow succeeded in refer-
ring to the trembling of Madame Hulot *as
if it were a thing with which we were familiar,*—"ce tremblement qui, depuis ce
moment, ne la quitta pas,"—as if we had all
known the lady in her later years, but had
not heard before how her infirmity first
came upon her.

But there is yet deeper meaning in the
scene. Madame Hulot's trembling-fit resulted, as one feels, from her recovery of her
mental stability at the expense of her nervous system. The energy which rushed to
her mind deserted her muscles. Balzac had
thought all this out; and in reading of it we
are moved not merely by his admirable
brevity of expression, but by the fundamen-
tal truth at the bottom of the whole matter.
An author of this sort is more god than artist. He trusts to his material: the saga will
deliver itself.

In the course of the same story the odious
retired shopkeeper, Crevel, announces that
he is going to marry the wicked adventuress
who is the destroyer of all the happiness of

BALZAC

his family. The family is outraged, and a
scene of general expostulation follows.

"La baronne fit un signe à la comtesse,
qui, prenant son enfant dans ses bras, lui dit :
'Allons, viens prendre ton bain, Wences-
las! Adieu, monsieur Crevel!'
La baronne salua Crevel en silence, et
Crevel ne put s'empêcher de sourire en
voyant l'étonnement de l'enfant quand il se
vit menacé de ce bain improvisé."

This astonishment of the child is as real and
as accidental to the reader as it was to Balzac himself.

Some years ago I went to a concert at St.
James's Hall in London. In one of the in-
termissions I recognised a very smart gentleman at whose house I had been fifteen years
before. I thought I would say how-d'-ye-do
to him, though I inwardly knew it would be
a foolish thing to attempt. I therefore approached him and made myself known, and
was shaken off in the approved London manner which was in fashion between the Fall
of Napoleon and the close of the Boer War.
As I sat thinking and wondering over this
rebuff, I observed another very smart gentleman approach the first, and the two shook

[237]

hands, saluted, dropped eye-glasses, cleared
their throats, and paused in the correct manner. In Elizabeth's time they would have
been slapping their thighs and swearing
the oaths of the season. Were they not two
bawcocks in excellent feather?

Yesterday I opened Balzac and read the
following description—which, by the way, is
dragged in by the heels, and has no dramatic
context:

"Le duc d'Hérouville, poli comme un
grand seigneur avec tout le monde, eut pour
le comte de la Palférine ce salut particulier
qui, sans accuser l'estime ou l'intimité, dit à
tout le monde: 'Nous sommes de la même
famille, de la même race, nous nous valons!'
Ce salut, le *siboleth* de l'aristocratie, à été
créé pour le désespoir des gens d'esprit de la
haute bourgeoisie."

Balzac, it will be noted, has explained the
psychology of the greetings, which remains
the same throughout the ages. He has
shown the part which the spectator plays in
the comedy. Is not this genius? Is not an
eye like this one of the great orbs of literature, and worthy to be named with the eye
of Aristotle or of Dante?

## BALZAC

At the opening of *Le Colonel Chabert* Balzac describes the entry of the destitute old Colonel into the clerks' room of a notary's office. The clerks are eating their improvised lunch and chatting. None of them has any attention to give to the stranger, and his knock, if he gave one, is not answered.

" 'Où est mon canif?'
'Je déjeune!'
'Va te faire lanlaire, voilà un pâté sur la requête!'
'Chut, messieurs!'
Ces diverses exclamations partirent à la fois au moment où le vieux plaideur ferma la porte avec cette sorte d'humilité qui dénature les mouvements de l'homme malheureux. L'inconnu essaya de sourire, mais les muscles de son visage se détendirent quand il eut vainement cherché quelques symptomes d'aménité sur les visages inexorablement insouciants des six clercs."

We see the poor outcast shutting the door in a never-to-be-forgotten attitude of abjection. He is soon dismissed amid the jeers of the company, after which the clerks fall into conversation about him.

" 'Ne voilà-t-il pas un fameux crâne?' dit Simonnin sans attendre que le vieillard eût fermé la porte.

'Il a l'air d'un déterré,' reprit le clerc.

'C'est quelque colonel qui réclame un arriéré,' dit le maître clerc.

'Non, c'est un ancien concierge,' dit Godeschal.

'Parions qu'il est noble,' s'écria Boucard.

'Je parie qu'il a été portier,' répliqua Godeschal. 'Les portiers sont seuls doués par la nature de carricks usés, huileux et déchiquetés par le bas comme l'est celui de ce vieux bonhomme. Vous n'avez donc vu ni ses bottes éculées qui prennent l'eau, ni sa cravate qui lui sert de chemise? Il a couché sous les ponts.'

'Il pourrait être noble et avoir tiré le cordon!' s'écria Desroches. 'Ça c'est vu.' "

The clerks determine to recall the old gentleman and ask him his name. Again he climbs the stairs and confronts his tormentors with humility. Balzac has enhanced the pathos of old Chabert's figure by this background which shows us the flippancy, the natural, unconscious cruelty of youth. The old man is dismissed at last, and there follows a description of the happy, aimless,

genial chatter of the clerks as they resume
their duties.  Finally Balzac says:

*"Cette scène représente un des mille plai-
sirs qui, plus tard, font dire en pensant à la
jeunesse:—C'était le bon temps."*

The italics are mine.  Here, by a momentary throb of feeling, Balzac has touched the
very nerve of truth.  Out of the sordid dust-
heap has sprung a flower.  These dreadful
clerks have opened a view into paradise.

At what moment, we ask ourselves, did
Balzac begin to vibrate with this lyric note,
so unexpectedly and so strongly struck?  If
it were Victor Hugo or Dickens we could
guess, but about Balzac we know nothing.

.    .    .    .    .    .    .

All this manner of procedure is very unlike the Gallic way of doing anything.  The
artistic vice of the French nation is a certain
virtuosity, which they love to throw into
everything they do.  I have seen a Frenchman play a Bach sonata for the violin, and
play it extremely well—but for the fact that
he seemed to be doing it with a foil.  He
wished us all to cry, "Touché!" at the finish.
The whole of French art and architecture,

French music, manners, and cookery, betray a delight in form for form's sake.

"S'il vous plait, madame!" says the farmer's daughter who has pushed a hand-cart of artichokes for nine miles to reach the gutter of the Rue St. Honoré; "s'il vous plait," she says to the frumpy old concierge, as she hands over the vegetables. "Merci, mademoiselle!" replies the concierge, giving some pennies. I have often wondered whether the excellent manners of the peasantry are not due to the Ancien Régime. The Revolution destroyed the nobles, but the peasantry picked up politeness from the aristocracy as they drove it towards the guillotine. I can hardly believe that the old *commères* in times before the Revolution called each other "madame." All this formalism is part of the play-instinct and of the æsthetic passion of the Ancien Régime. It is a part of that external grace which made life beautiful and turned every avocation into an art.

Such was the gift of Old France to the world: her nobles invented napkins and *boutonnières* and a good way of doing everything; and most of the social civilisation that we know is due to France's love of form. The old French monarchy, from Louis XIII

# BALZAC

to Louis XVI, was the central social bureau
for humanity, and taught everyone the
proper way of writing, building, thinking,
standing, complimenting, fighting, and living.

This belief that form is an essential to
all kinds of conduct is, of course, ever a little at war with the individual. The greatest
writers of France, whether they lived before
or after the classic period, have not always
shared the conventional French spirit. Montaigne, Rabelais, the Duc de Saint-Simon,
and Balzac are writers of a popular school,
indulging at will in vulgarisms and expressing themselves with a sort of mediæval freedom which resembles the English rather than
the French way of writing. All four of
them despise the academic spirit, and run
about like colts. To those Frenchmen who
accept their own classic tradition, the writers I have named savour a little of barbar-
ism; to men of other nationalities these
barbarians of France are the only writers of
France who are quite free from the curling-
tongs.

Balzac is completely outside the frame of
national correctness, and his language, as
even a foreigner can feel, is academically
outrageous. He is of the people, he is a man

[ 243 ]

of genius, he is unconscious, indifferent,
preoccupied, whirled away in a chariot
drawn by dragons. He is well fed, familiar,
serious. He talks with the mouths of fifty
dialects, with the slangs of every province
and every *arrondissement,* with the pretensions and educational imperfections peculiar
to each of his two thousand characters, with
the exuberance of a gigantic nature. What,
then, has become of the Academy? The
Academy must be picked out of the débris,
if the fragments can be found. Balzac up-
sets the apple-cart of French classicism, and
in doing so he makes the strongest com-
mentary on it that has ever been made.
Without such an upsetting there could have
been no Balzac.

The dream that Balzac dreamed was not
a tale or a series of tales; it was a society, or,
more accurately speaking, a mythology.
Instead of taking fifty characters, as the
Greeks did, and writing plays about the
dramatic moments in their lives, Balzac
takes a whole epoch—and a very brilliant,
topsyturvy epoch—and carries in his head
the lives of all its inhabitants from youth to
old age. Roughly speaking, this epoch was
his own time, and it was, I suppose, the most
dramatic epoch in history. If you will read

BALZAC

in M. Lenôtre's works those sketches of the
odd personalities which came to the top in
the Revolution, you will find more samples
of incredible transformation, more varieties
of fantastic change in rôle, than you could
easily dig up out of the rest of the memoirs
of Europe. The rise of the Napoleonic
world, the fall of the ancient kingdom, the
purgatorial and infernal interval of the Revolution which connected these two eras,
would have been enough for Dante. But
Balzac had also the Restoration to draw on,
and the age of Louis Philippe. I suppose
that one could hardly put one's hand on a
Frenchman, of whatever caste or class, born
in 1780 and who survived until 1850, whose
life would not show changes, powerfully coloured and filled with frantic interest for a
novelist. Balzac perceived this in his earliest
years, and filled his mind with typical biog-
raphies—of personages already costumed
and documented, who lived in the closet of
his mind, ready to walk on the stage of his
fiction; men with ancestors and family his-
tories, and with private lives that are full of
kaleidoscopic change. They are the citizens
of the imaginative world where Balzac himself lived. If the story in hand needs a
notary or a senator or a Napoleonic general,

# GREEK GENIUS

a Jewish banker, a hangman's clerk, Balzac
already has the man in his greenroom.  He
does not have to create him, as every other
novelist must do; he simply refers to him—
taps a bell, and in he walks.  The wonderful
single-phrase descriptions which gleam on
every page of the novels owe their brilliancy
to this familiarity of the author with his
characters.

Balzac was a philosopher, and he had been
laying up observation, as the bee lays up
honey, for years.  His tale is a demonstration; it is a stair to some thought; it exists
not for its own sake, but for the sake of re-
moter truth; it is an illustration and a
parable.  Old thoughts, observations made
long ago, the wine that has lain for nine
years in the cellar, types seen, philosophies
guessed at, beliefs that are older than the
work in hand, but leap out upon the work in
hand as fire leaps towards the electric needle
—these things are what give life and felicity
to his vehicle.

The vehicle was the *Comédie Humaine,*
as he assembled it in his own mind.  Here
he created for himself a language that could
say anything.  The characters themselves
are not men, but projections of thought; the
colours in them result from the analysis of

light. Colours made in this way are the only
colours that will hold; for colours that are
ignorantly copied out of nature soon fade
into nondescript. There is nothing in Balzac which is copied from nature. Everything has been first understood and then
arranged so as to symbolise nature. There
is nothing in Balzac that is not based on sane
speculation, or that will not go back into the
ten commandments. There is nothing that
exists merely for the sake of the picturesque.
Everything has been drenched in meaning.

That it means so much to us who have no
part or lot in it is proof that this world of
Balzac's is a world of myth. These weird
creatures of Balzac's brain—Rastignac,
Goriot, Nucingen, Grandet—are not of the
actual world. They are Gothic extravagances. Time may turn them into caricatures, as time has begun to do with the
creations of Dickens and Victor Hugo, but
as yet the figures of Balzac are thrilling real-
ities—unreal in form, true in substance, and
among the most moving creations of human
wit.

The difference between him and other
writers of fiction is that he did not wait for
a story, but created a miniature world in
which his stories are all related to one an-

other. He is not content that a novel shall
be a unity. A novel is only a spoke in the
wheel of his unity. Each novel is a fragment, and yet it is as big as the Coliseum,
and is meant to suggest the larger world of
thought in which Balzac himself is living.
He succeeds in this ambition, this desire to
make us feel that all these characters and
dramas are parts of something else; and in
this he resembles Dante. Every line in Balzac bears a living relation to every other
line. We cannot know just what that relation is, but we feel that there is a connection.
It is as if we were walking on the surface of
some sphere and had gained a conviction as
to the size and sweep of it through our feet.

Balzac seems to be like Rembrandt and
Shakespeare in that he is always Balzac, and
yet he never does the same thing twice. He
is always experimenting. He lives for himself. He somehow housed the dream of his
existence in his characters. He always
maintained that his writings were but pages
out of one great book. It is the triumph
of contemplation.

He has, as it were, no outer life: he is all
artist. His works are not really works at
all, but are what is left over in the mere
process of the artist's existence. In making

BALZAC

them he is experiencing, he is searching.
One cannot tell how much is improvisation
and how much is calculation in Balzac. He
will often preach extempore for thirty sec-
onds, and then go on describing accessories,
like a stage carpenter, for half an hour. He
is almost devoid of virtuosity. I must admit
that sometimes, in a preface, he parades the
number of books he has read; and that we
know he was amazed at his own talent and
thought himself as great as Napoleon. But
this impinging of his self-consciousness upon
the field of his work is very rare.

The gloom of Balzac is against him, to
my mind; it is a weakness. If he were still
greater than he is, he would be more cheerful. But let us consider his dark, peculiar
mood.

Balzac, like Dante, suffers from a lack of
humour; but one feels the absolute benevolence of Balzac, whereas we know that
Dante's benevolence is cut into by political
hatreds and by petty theological dogmas.
Dante is not a good fellow, but Balzac is as
warm as the sun. The young person will
not feel this warmth; for Balzac's fondness
for shadows, his love of accumulating dam-
nations and allowing them to rain and pour
down the pit into the infernal regions below,

sweeping virtuous persons along with them,
is unpleasing and confusing to the conscience of the young. His almost exclusive
interest in the forces which grind downward
is a weakness. There are forces in the universe which grind upward, bringing good
out of evil and peace out of sin. Why could
not Balzac have given us pictures of these
heaven-ascending and angelic powers more
frequently than he did? Thus reasons
youth, and I sympathise with it; but as one
grows older and becomes more astute, one
perceives that there is a large element of the
conventional, of the intellectual, of the
purely æsthetic, in Balzac's tragedies. We
must not weep too hard over the pains of
the virtuous in Balzac, over the Goriots and
the Madame Hulots—no, nor even over the
punishment of the wicked. All these personages are symbols, and we gradually come
to feel more distinctly the goodness and
purity of the great brain and the great heart
that have set these symbols in motion. I
suppose there does not exist in the world a
more powerful picture of domestic infelicity
than Balzac gives in describing the Hulot
family in *La Cousine Bette*. The tragedy is
set forth with the remorselessness of mathe-
matics and the power of Niagara. It is

painful, it is horrible.  One wonders how an
author can bear to depict misery at such
length and in such detail.  But in the midst
of the whole relation—that is to say, at
about two hundred and fifty octavo pages
from the beginning of the tale, and one hundred and fifty before the end—Balzac casts
in the following sturdy, sensible, unemo-
tional paragraph, which explains his relation to the whole matter:

"Cette esquisse permet aux âmes inno-
centes de deviner les differents ravages que
les madame Marneffe exercent dans les fa-
milles, et par quels moyens elles atteignent
de pauvres femmes vertueuses, en apparence
si loin d'elles.  Mais, si l'on veut transporter
par la pensée ces troubles à l'étage supérieur
de la société, près du trône; en voyant ce
que doivent avoir coûté les maîtresses des
rois, on mesure l'étendue des obligations du
peuple envers ses souverains quand ils don-
nent l'exemple des bonnes mœurs et de la
vie de famille."

There is a benevolent-thinking person outside the phantasmagoria of the *Comédie Humaine*—and the sensibleness and *bonhomie*

of this great heart is what blesses the *Co-médie*.

There is another element to be considered. In studying the shadows in any tragic art we must take account of tradition. Achilles must die: Fate claims him. The child in the audience cries when he first understands this; and the unsophisticated are made to suffer by the cruelties of art. The inhabitants of the Mediterranean, on the other hand, frankly enjoy tragedy, because they invented it; they know it is a sham, a mere idea-in-action. Now the French possess a bit of coast on the Mediterranean which, in spite of the fun the Parisians make of its inhabitants, is the most important fact in French history, and has controlled the development of French art in all its forms. The Frenchman is a more intellectual being than the Saxon or the Angle. He does not enjoy a joke against himself, but he enjoys a tragedy against himself, if it is a good tragedy. The Comte de Ségur, aide-de-camp to Napoleon, saw the retreat from Moscow with the eyes of Thucydides. Neither his admiration for Napoleon, on the one hand, nor his sorrow in France's downfall, on the other, beclouds the judgment of the young writer. He speaks as a pure in-

telligence, and he perceives the magnificent
tragic elements which ruled the entire drama
of the retreat. In the same spirit Victor
Hugo described Waterloo, and Zola described the Franco-German War. No English, German, or American man of letters,
in dealing with the misfortunes of his country, could display an intellectual detachment
of this sort. His self-consciousness would
be too great, and his æsthetic interest too
feeble, to permit of his describing a national
catastrophe,—no matter how magnificent,—
with artistic zeal.

There is in Balzac a meridional feeling
that tragedy must be tragic. If a woman is
to sacrifice life and honour, she must not
merely go to the brink and then be saved
through a trick of the plot: she must go to
the bottom. If a man is to die of drink, he
must be reduced to the meanest attic by
*delirium tremens,* and his children must beg
their bread. There is a non-sentimental,
workmanlike thoroughness in this march
of evil that hurts the feelings of Anglo-
Saxons, who cannot accept these matters
as good symbolism and telling art, but keep
on being sorry that Achilles must die.

I suggest this view of Balzac's dark and
tragic tendencies the rather that I find my-

self less offended by his gloom the older I
grow. It becomes ever more clear to me
that Balzac's melancholy is the melancholy
of the artist, not of the cynic. It is poetic
melancholy, and his tragedy is largely conventional, as all good tragedy ought to be.

There is a secret about all great art, and
the secret is as profound in the case of writing as in the case of music. The power that
holds us is something deeper than all explanation, than all criticism. The world contains not only death-chairs, which kill men
through a low and alternating electric current, but life-chairs, which vitalise men
through an exceedingly high and perfectly
steady current, and the experience in each
case is unconscious. We step into the vortex, the power is turned on, and something
happens which controls and changes us.

Balzac is such a life-chair. People seek
him for various reasons. Many read him
for the story. They plunge into the unend-
ing romance of him, just as the mediæval
reader plunged into *The Romaunt of the
Rose;* others read Balzac for his pictures of
manners, or of character, or for his wise
remarks on life. Still others read him in
search of metaphysical ideas. These are
often distressed by the tale and indifferent to

the fate of its characters; yet they are held
to the task of understanding it, they must
know what Balzac is driving at. I myself
often finish a book of Balzac's almost wish-
ing that I had never begun it. His books
add a new duty to life. To read one of them
is like having a live crab entangled in one's
hair: there is no quick way of getting him
out.

And yet perhaps all of these various
kinds of readers are brothers in destiny. The
interest of the story, the descriptions of
manners, the philosophic appeal, are all
merely baits that lead different men to put
their necks into the collar, or to sit in the
life-chair. The books begin lumberingly;
and then, suddenly, we are caught, we are in
the throes, we are under the waves. Our
brains have been brought into contact with
a big dynamic thinking apparatus which con-
nects us with the maelstrom of infinity.

We should use no method in dealing with
Balzac, but should approach him through
accident and chaotically, pulling down one
of his books occasionally to see if it speaks
to us. The scholars have tried to measure
him. They have walked over his huge back
like inch-worms. Even Sainte-Beuve, the

most liberal of the Frenchmen, tries to
"place" Balzac. But the jug is too wide for
the shelf : the critic is left with the sprawling
author in his arms.

One should not try to know one's Balzac
nor feel any responsibility towards him. His
merits dodge the searchlight and thereafter
walk abroad in the dusk, like shy leopards
with velvet feet. You cannot be sure of
finding them or of showing them to another ;
they are intimate and personal things. Those
happy words, odd hints and phrases, in Balzac are part of the great unspoken, moving
drama at the back of his mind. They live in
a space of three dimensions, and we cannot
get them to stick upon our flat page.

The other day I opened the *Médecin de
Campagne* with innocence, because I had
never heard of it. During the first twenty-
five pages I became bored, because I had
hoped for a detective story, and the thing
seemed to be turning into a didactic romance
about the good citizen. I had dreadful
recollections of Harriet Martineau's tales,
and the teaching of economic truth through
fiction. The scheme of the book is to suggest that a single man may transform a
whole countryside from a wilderness to a
paradise in the course of a few years. The

## BALZAC

*Médecin de Campagne* is a saint, but a new
kind of saint—a social worker. I was
browsing my way through the book when I
came across a thought that was familiar,—
namely, that the defective classes are a
source of piety.

"Admirable religion! elle a placé les
secours d'une bienfaisance aveugle près
d'une aveugle infortune.   Là où se trouvent
des crétins, la population croit que la pré-
sence d'un être de cette espèce porte bonheur
à la famille.   Cette croyance sert à rendre
douce une vie qui, dans le sein des villes,
serait condamnée aux rigueurs d'un fausse
philanthropie et à la discipline d'un hospice.
Dans la vallée supérieure de l'Isère, où ils
abondent, les crétins vivent en plein air avec
les troupeaux qu'ils sont dressés à garder.
Au moins sont-ils libres et respectés comme
doit l'être le malheur."

This passage would have passed over me as
a commonplace reflection, but that I happened to be familiar with the life and writings of Dr. Samuel Gridley Howe, the great
American philanthropist, who began his life
as a Philhellene in Byron's time, became
famous at a later date through teaching

deaf-mutes to read and write, and ended his life as the patriarch of every form of beneficence. Now Dr. Howe disapproved of confining the defective classes in institutions. He believed in leaving them with their families, or in farming them out among kind people in the country. I have read eloquent reports made by Dr. Howe at the time he was at the head of all the charities of Massachusetts (that is to say, about 1865–1875), which are no more than disquisitions on the words of Balzac which I have quoted. Was Balzac in 1835 familiar with the advanced scientific theories of criminology which Dr. Howe put into practice in 1875? Or did Balzac, through a mere act of intuition in imagining a modern saint, arrive at certain ideas peculiar to Howe, who was a typical modern saint? Balzac gives the elements of the modern citizen-saint much as a mathematician might give the solution of a problem. This whole story suggests Howe.

Balzac seems to be able to manufacture humanity; he uses live creatures to state his thought. When you or I write an essay, a sermon, or a treatise, we deduce arguments and weave a net of ideas. All these ideas are portions of humanity, and could really

exist only in live men. Balzac knows this,
and knows it so well that the ideas are not
true to him, ideas are not ideas at all unless
they are seen as living characters. He
thinks in characters, as the dramatists do.
His power of thought is so comprehensive
that it makes things vibrate far and near.
Before he has done with a subject the idea
has been put into a shape where it seems to
be an ineradicable living verity, a part of
humanity, true for yesterday, true for Pata-
gonia and for Massachusetts and for 1950.

M. Faguet says very decisively that Balzac is no thinker; but that is because the
stage of Balzac's thought is so immense that
M. Faguet does not feel that he is in a theatre at all. No one has taken his tickets.
The Three Fatal Judges of the Underworld,
who sit with red ribbons in the lapels of
their evening coats in the foyer of the Français, are not seen in Balzac. "Bah!" says
the Académicien, "this is no theatre: it is a
Bartholomew fair!"

Whether it be a fair or a theatre, the
mimic world of Balzac is a world of symbolism, ruled by certain laws of illusion, and it
is in his subtle handling of these laws that
he excels. The money on the stage is never
real; and so with all the sham doors an

false situations in fiction—there is the magic of ideas in all of them, and we must leave this magic in its place. It will not do to transport a bit of the theatre or a scene out of a story into the actual world. We must not try to match up a piece of the imaginative world with its analogue in real life. The thing is merely a symbol, and has no analogue. The great creators produce in us an illusion of their omniscience. The poet is a kind of god; the novelist seems to know the whole of life. Balzac appears to comprehend politics, art, finance, bric-à-brac, the wine trade, peasant life, student life, provincial life, the Church,—everything. He creates in us a most vivid belief that he understands all things.

But of course Balzac knew none of these things correctly; he merely knew their stage uses, their imaginative values, their symbolic effectivenesses. It will not do for us to catechise him about the Catholic Church, or about the Bourbon Monarchy, or about universal suffrage. Down to 1845 he had never been in a law court: "je n'avais jamais entendu plaider." He wandered into the Cour d'Assises, and was so interested that he remained there all day. This romancer who, one might say, first discovered

the dramatic value of the law and of law-
suits in fiction, knows nothing of law. He
can improvise it as fast as he needs it. Improvise? No, not quite that, but pick it out
of a book, or a friend, or the gutter. He
lays his hand on some old leather rag of
reality and turns it into a king's mantle in his
story-book.

Balzac's Pickwickian expedition to Sar-
dinia, which in 1838 he visited alone and in
secret for the sake of discovering the silver-
mines left by the Romans, exhibits more
kinds of ignorance of the world than were
ever brought together before. His secretive-
ness and his cunning, his enthusiasm for
science, his lust for gold, his fatiguing journeys, his maddening quarantines,—all the
sufferings of the Parisian Balzac, who
found himself "dans un désert rempli d'in-
connus quasi-sauvages,"—are described in
letters which seem like screams of pain:

"J'ai traversé une forêt vierge penché sur
le cou de mon cheval sous peine de la vie;
car, pour la traverser, il fallait marcher dans
un cours d'eau, couvert d'un berceau de
plantes grimpantes et de branches qui m'au-
raient éborgné, cassé les dents, emporté la
tête. C'est des chênes verts gigantesques,

des arbres à liége, des lauriers, des bruyères
de trente pieds de hauteur. Rien à manger."

This Sardinian episode of Balzac's life,
though it is told in only twenty pages of
print, is as remarkable as Daudet's *Tartarin*
—which, by the way, it vividly recalls.

The passion for finance, which makes the
money-matters in his books so real and so
thrilling, ruined Balzac in real life. In this
department he seems to have transplanted
his stage beliefs into the actual world, and
something of the same sort is true of his
love-affairs. He had an uncertain comprehension of the woman he loved. This artist,
who knew women better than any artist
since Euripides (I have heard young women
declare that they generally shut all the doors
when they sit down to read Balzac),—this
master of the soul of women in fiction,—
seems to have lived in a region of half-com-
prehension with regard to Madame Hanska,
the woman he loved for eighteen years.

With the exception of finance and of
Madame Hanska, he had no interest in the
actual. His art consumed him. It trans-
lated all actualities into fiction so fast that
you might say that for him the world had no
charms, no terrors. He simplified his life

# BALZAC

to a mere desk in a cottage, and would have been completely happy but for the incursion of his symbolic world of finance and of his symbolic world of love into this cottage.

Madame Hanska was astonished that Balzac, who knew the criminal classes so well, should often be a prey to sharpers. She asks him how it is possible that he should be an innocent. He pleads that fatigue and distraction are the cause of it, that Napoleon cannot be in all places at once, and so forth. But the real reason he does not suspect,— namely, that the thieves' world of fiction is not the real thieves' world, and that the great creator of criminals in fiction does not recognise a criminal in the street.

This is as it must be, and we ought not to be astonished. Life is so complex that any one aspect of it is enough to occupy and exhaust the greatest intellect. The poet, the banker, the economist, the physicist has all he can master if he knows the dialect of his own province of the mind.

The great and insoluble question with Balzac is, of course, the same as it is with Shakespeare and with Dickens, How do the characters get into the poet? How do Falstaff and Mrs. Gamp come to exist? and do observation and study have much to do with the matter? There are two or three chance sentences in Balzac's letters which throw more light on the subject than all that the critics have said from the age of Aristotle downward.

In writing to Madame Hanska, he says that he drew his women from his imagination, and did not copy them from his acquaintances. He says this in answer to a letter in which she had evidently twitted him for his intimate knowledge of women, and called him a lady-killer. Again, to the Duchesse d'Abrantès, who had raised the same question in a wider form, he describes the spontaneous play of ideas that went on in his mind, and which made him feel like a bystander, and adds:

"Ce kaléidoscope-là vient-il de ce que, dans l'âme de ceux qui pretendent vouloir peindre toutes les affections et le cœur humain, le hasard jette toutes les affections mêmes, afin qu'ils puissent, par la force de leur imagination, ressentir ce qu'ils peignent? *et l'observation ne serait-elle qu'une sorte de mémoire propre à aider cette mobile imagination?* Je commence à le croire."

The italics are mine. Here is a statement by

BALZAC

one of the few great geniuses who are competent to speak; and he seems to say that his external observation of men is merely an aid to his internal memory; that is, it helps to catch and docket the characters that seethe within his imagination. Perhaps this is as clear a statement as we may ever expect to receive upon the matter. The words show the extent to which the external world is subjected to the internal in the mind of an artist.

In modern times it is customary to talk about the "message" of an artist, but no one has ever discovered what the term means. The mind of an artist is normally a blank, except where his art fills it in, and those who create the strongest illusion of omniscience are probably the most completely ignorant of things not within their craft. Take away his ink-pot or his paint-box, and the artist is a fish out of water. His life is in the hieroglyphics of his trade. This is his message; this is himself. The greater the poet, the less is he conscious of any message, because the less is he aware of the actual world. He has transhumanised everything he knows to suit his own temperament. Small natures, who live half in the real world and half in their own peculiar moods, are burdened with a sense of message. I cannot find that Balzac had any conscious message. He wanted fame; he needed money; he wrote furiously. The rest was consequence. The whole was destiny.

There are certain critics whose *forte* it is to complain that the great masters did n't really know their own business. Critics of this sort rule the whole literature of painting, and abound in all other literatures; and it is no wonder if certain students have fallen foul of Balzac on the ground that he is not sufficiently literate. M. Faguet says that the novelist was not a reader. But if you turn to Balzac's letters you find that the artist had, after all, some reading. He mentions Sterne, Mirabeau, La Fontaine, Rousseau, de Staël, Voltaire, Richardson, Juvenal, Rabelais, Goethe, Byron, etc., etc., with the sort of freedom that educated persons use; and the range of his allusions is wide. His historical novels and his philosophical romances imply reading. He owned ten thousand volumes, and refused to give up his library to his creditors on the ground that his books were the tools of his trade. He constantly asks his mother to procure particular books for him.

# BALZAC

It is, indeed, impossible for any great literary man not to be bookish. From Dante and Petrarch downward, all the great poets and writers have been bookish; they have lived on books as the seal lives on fish. The passion for reading is the one quality that great literary men have in common with small literary men. The difference seems to be that books feed the great ones and poison the small ones.

Balzac is a great *jongleur* who draws upon an inexhaustible repertory of tales, and weaves many threads from the past into his great tapestries. His manner of treating the romance is the correct, traditional manner, which has survived from the days of Miletus because it is popular and agreeable. The *genre* of romance-writing permits and invites this discursive method; and persons who would divide fiction into (1) narrative, (2) discursive, etc., are, from an academic point of view, entirely in the wrong. It is their own reading, not Balzac's reading that has been narrow. Balzac had no *esthétique*,—that is, he had no formula, —but he had practices. He did what Homer and Ovid and their mediæval and modern successors have always done. Chaucer, Cervantes, Scott, and Balzac, with all their discursiveness, belong to the school which seduces and enchants. The asides and excursions in Balzac interest us as much as the story. And besides, they are a part of the story; they are swirling portions of the great river.

As the "message" of the artist must be left in limbo, so the "philosophy" of a poet ought to be liberally treated. In dealing with it we must content ourselves with allusions—pointing to the thought, but never attempting to extract, define, or reproduce it. We are all in search of the poet's idea— we who read his books and feel his power. Every work of art carries a philosophy in its hand. There is a metaphysic even in Shakespeare and Walter Scott; and there is in Balzac a far more approachable mode of thought than in either of these.

When Balzac was in his teens, he had visions of becoming a philosopher. He wrote a *Théorie de la Volonté*, which, to his lasting regret, was burned by an ignorant teacher. He mourned the loss, for he thought that this early work would have shown the world what talents he had in the field of metaphysics. Nevertheless, as he turned from philosophy to romance, as he dropped the ferule and took up the wand, the

*Théorie de la Volonté* still haunted his thought. There is an ever-present metaphysic in Balzac, a thing peculiar to his mind, and unitary; that is to say, consistent with itself, philosophical. It is a general conception of life as force, and of the visible portions of our being as mere projections of the far larger and more important invisible parts. This conception is what gives brilliancy, transparency, enduring power to his fiction. In the author's mind the externals are mere lenses, reflecting surfaces, reverberations which voice an invisible drama that is conducted by the gods above. The life lies behind and beyond. The future is always present, and the past is present; the story is a philosophical romance.

This point of view is conveyed by a thousand hints, and sometimes by discourses, as in the *Peau de Chagrin,* in *Le Cousin Pons* (the discourse on fortune-telling), in the *Recherche de l'Absolu,* etc., etc. The thought itself can live only in a half-light, and Balzac is happiest in dealing with it by asides. When he becomes dogmatic and heavy,—as, for instance, in *Seraphita* and in *Louis Lambert,*—when he determines to be a philosopher and swears he will force his idea down the throat of the world, he becomes deadly and inexpressive. Good Lord, deliver us from him!

But the mysticism of Balzac, when it appears as a mere illumination due to vision— like the aura of the saints—is the divine power in him, divinely working, divinely seeing. The introduction by him of this element—I should say the perception by him of this element—at work in the midst of the most real realism, the realism invented by the father of realism, is what gives its character to the *Comédie Humaine*.

In his great tragic romances the track of some mighty egoism is followed across society. Ambition, avarice, envy, misguided love, unbridled sensuality, are so depicted that we feel them to be the visitations of madness, foci of inscrutable, compelling force, which wreck the lives of many and ravage the world like a disease. Not since Shakespeare's two or three greatest tragedies has there been any human writing so powerfully and completely tragic as these books. They leave us with a sense of reality with which no fiction competes.

These great tragedies are merely monuments which stand out in the city of Balzac's literature. They themselves differ greatly

from one another, and cannot be reduced to
a formula, for each one of them is vitalised
by a principle which is peculiar to itself.
The merits of the lesser works are also so
interwoven with their substance that criticism cannot name them exactly. Life leaps
from the pages—that is all we know.

The *Peau de Chagrin* is a book full of
*longueurs;* but it contains an unforgettable
idea, and the story passes from plain tale
into allegory and back again without transition. The story glows and throbs with
truth, because life also vibrates between the
actual and the metaphysical. The most
solid houses are constantly melting into mist
as we gaze on them. How often do we see
sky and sea, hopes, dreams, and fears, shine
through the solid masonry about us! Things
good and bad, great and small, get at us
through the bars and bonds of time. In Balzac everything glows; there is a glamour
and a novelty about his scenes which are like
the hopes of youth and the foretaste of happiness. Everything is thrilling, rich, clear,
certain, and inevitable. The *Arabian Nights*
are not more satisfying to the romantic ap-
petite. You feel the completeness of the
tale; you repose in its fatality from the beginning. To what extent are his stories

spontaneous, to what extent arranged? I
do not know.   But I know that they are
studied things, like good music; they are artificial, symbolic things; they are abstractions; there is algebra concealed in them.

Like all powerful forms of art, these tales
are complex centres where many and various
kinds of force converge and are superposed
one upon the other.   The same tale often
has the interest of a detective story, of a
melodrama, an allegory, a picture of manners, and of a personal letter from Balzac.
This multiplicity of content is what makes a
writer great, for it is a quality which we do
not outgrow.   If we tire of the theme, we
enjoy the construction.   At twenty we love
the villain, at forty the epilogue.   This complexity of idea is what gives to any work
the quality of pure intellect.

To take an example: the Russian novels
are much simpler in content than Balzac's
novels.   They are exhaustible: we tire of
them.   They are written by men whose
minds have not been subdued by the classic
traditions of Western Europe; by men who
are not hooped in and controlled by conventional æsthetic standards.   The Russian
novels do not contain a tincture of the *Arabian Nights,* and of Boccaccio, and of

*Clarissa Harlowe,* as Balzac does. They lack a hundred elements which go to make up fiction. The art that soothes us, makes us happy, gives us the truth, is the art that conveys an abstraction and leaves no problem behind.

Mere pictures of manners and of politics, mere moralities and economic tales, mere social studies, no matter how true or how deserving, are parts of the raw material of life. They belong to the crude ore which we all have to deal with in our own work-shops. I am not willing to give my painful attention to reading a novel if the book is only a restatement of life's injustices and incongruities, a mere attack on the incomprehensibility of the universe. I must have something that gives me a clue or a sense of solution, something that confirms the faith in me which the real world so constantly baffles. This is what great works of art do for us.

It is a wonderful proof of the ultimate identity of comedy and tragedy that Balzac, whom most people would name as the greatest modern tragedian, was in his person the very ideal of a comic poet. He was the god Pan in the flesh. His lips curved, his brow bulged, his eyes gleamed, his fingers played the pipe. There were reeds in his hair; his garments were mere drapery; his good humour and natural honour, and his inexhaustible fountains of life, courage, benevolence, deluged those who saw him, and live yet in the pictures of him and in his letters, which add the last and greatest figure to Balzac's gallery,—to wit, the figure of Balzac himself.

The externals of this deity are as simple as those of some demigod to whom the decorative arts have assigned but one symbol. Balzac's symbol is a dressing-gown. He has no home, family, wife, fortune, circle, career, or periods of life. He got into debt in his early youth, and remained in debt. He changed his lodgings, but never his mind. His temperament added to his debt faster than his talent could diminish it; and so it went—more debt, more fiction—till the end.

· · · · · ·

Balzac was born in Tours in 1799, and at twelve years of age moved to Paris with his family. He died in 1850, having written about a hundred books, large and small. He was a short, stout man with a beaming face and nature,—beaming, that is, except when he was in the glooms from exhaustion and

BALZAC

overwork.  His manner of life and his method of composition are deeply related to his art.  They were the habits of the brilliant crammer, who sits up all night with a wet towel round his head, and does the work of a half-year in twelve hours.  Only with Balzac the work began at midnight and lasted till five o'clock on the following afternoon; and the *régime* was kept up for several months at a time.  As for food, he ate when he pleased, except that he seems to have dined regularly and dined early.  This way of life did not result in killing him till he was fifty-one, because, in the first place, he had the strongest constitution imaginable, and secondly, because he had no dissipations, used no drugs or alcohol, his only vice being black coffee, which occasionally he would forswear.  It must be observed, also, as a thing of the very greatest importance, that his sleeping hours were the early hours of the night—from seven to twelve.

In 1838, after this outrageous *régime* had been in operation for ten or twelve years, he writes:

"Comme j'avais été vingt-cinq jours sans dormir, je suis, depuis un mois, occupé à dormir quinze ou seize heures par jour et à

[275]

ne rien faire pendant les huit heures de
vieille; je me refais de la cervelle pour la
dépenser à mesure qu'elle vient."

This power of sleep is proof that Balzac's
nature was still intact.

The way of life, however, made a recluse
of him. He had the concentration, the mental isolation of an astronomer. His original
qualities,—his ingenuousness, his unworld-
liness, were no doubt intensified by his seclu-
sion. As a boy he shut himself up to work
off a debt, and at the age of fifty-one he
walked out of his study into his grave, and
had lost none of his ideals.

The privacy of his life had, I believe, a
good deal to do with this retention of his
youth, both in a good sense and a bad one.
He was an ingenuous, high-strung creature.
The following passage is not a page from
Goethe's *Werther,* nor a page out of the
diary of an *ingénue* in one of George Sand's
romances. It is part of a letter written by
Balzac, at the age of thirty-nine, to Madame
Hanska, whom he had known in Vienna
some years before. He writes from Milan:

"Je suis allé à la poste pour savoir si
quelqu'un aurait eu l'idée de m'écrire poste

restante. J'ai trouvé une lettre de la comtesse Thürhein, qui vous aimait tant et que
vous aimiez aussi, et où votre nom était pro-
noncé au milieu d'une phrase mélancolique
qui m'a ému profondément; . . . Je me
suis assis sur un banc et suis resté près d'une
heure les yeux attachés sur le Duomo, fas-
ciné par tout ce que cette lettre rappelait. Et
tous les incidents de mon séjour à Vienne
ont passé devant moi dans toute leur vérité
naïve, dans toute leur candeur de marbre.
Ah! que ne doit-on pas, je ne dis pas à
celle qui nous cause de si douces et pures
souvenances, mais au fragile papier qui les
réveille."

This passage may be taken as the keystone
in the long arch of his passion for her, which
began in 1833 and ended only with his life.

This retirement and perpetual contemplation kept the bloom on his feelings, yet it
kept him also in prey to his moods. Towards the end of his life he became more
and more excessive in his exaltations and in
his depressions. The insanity of the lover,
which is pleasing in the boy of nineteen,
gives us concern in the man of fifty. Balzac
thinks of his mistress every hour; he walks

into churches and kneels before altars and prays for her; she is his ever-present deity.

In 1846 he receives a cruel letter. Its early pages cause him so much anguish that, dropping it unfinished, he rushes up the Rue de Rivoli in his summer shoes, though the snow is ankle-deep. His aspect alarms what friends he meets. He plods the boulevards all day, and, returning exhausted to his home in Passy at ten o'clock at night, he flings himself into bed. But sleep deserts his eyelids. He therefore rises, lights his fire as well as the fifty candles of his bronze chandelier, and proceeds to finish the letter, whose balmy final passages somewhat assuage the sufferings which its earlier pages have caused.

A man of this kind is a good lover but a bad companion, and we must regard it as fortunate that circumstances compelled him to live apart from the object of his adoration, except for the many journeys taken together and the many visits which the lovers paid to each other in Poland and in France. One feels convinced that there was less suffering in Balzac's life than if his marriage with Madame Hanska had taken place at an earlier date.

The negative portrait of this woman

# BALZAC

which comes to us out of Balzac's letters to
her is not reassuring. We get an impression
that she was at times bored by his assidui-
ties, that she sometimes played upon his feelings, that she made use of him to collect
autographs, that she was somehow a vulgar-
minded person. We must not forget, however, that she completely satisfied Balzac's
romanticism and perfected his life, and that
she finally did, in obedience to Russian law,
give up her fortune in order to marry him.
Her husband died in 1841 : she married Balzac in 1850.

A disillusionment of some sort seems to
have fallen upon the lovers soon after their
marriage; both of them were no longer
young, and both were very ill. Certainly
their wedding journey from Poland to Paris
is one of the saddest in history.

I should be content if not quite so many
of Balzac's letters to Madame Hanska had
survived. A *liaison* carried on by corre-
spondence, which continues for eighteen
years, becomes an integral part of two lives.
The people become necessary to each other,
and this fact is more important than anything which they say in their letters. The
letters are the ceaseless drumming of the
mill-wheels of life.

Your complete literary man writes all the time. It wakes him in the morning to write, it exercises him to write, it rests him to write. Writing is to him a visit from a friend, a cup of tea, a game of cards, a walk in the country, a warm bath, an after-dinner nap, a hot Scotch before bed, and the sleep that follows it. Your complete literary chap is a writing animal; and when he dies he leaves a cocoon as large as a haystack, in which every breath he has drawn is recorded in writing. We must place these cocoons in our cabinet, but we need not label them with very lofty names, even though some great butterflies have flown out of them. There are men and women, great and small, who have left a wilderness of memorials behind them. We feel that we should know them better if we did not know so much about them. The Carlyles were distinguished figures before their memoirs were published. Balzac's letters to Madame Hanska belong to this crushing class, which here encloses, as it often does, an enormous interest. The interest in this case comes from discovering that all we had guessed about Balzac in reading the novels is proved to be true by the letters.

There is no night side to Balzac's life or

nature—a thing which the world has been
slow to believe. Most great sentimentalists,
like Goethe, Byron, de Musset, have at one
time or another been dissipated men, a thing
which shows in their philosophy and in their
artistic work. Balzac seems to have had no
period of dissipation. I do not mean that
he was irreproachably virtuous, but that he
retained throughout life an innocence of
feeling which is foreign to Gallic sentiment.
At the risk of making the reader laugh, I
must give a portion of an indignant letter
which Balzac writes in 1832 to one of his
oldest friends, Madame Carraud, who had
suggested to him a worldly marriage:

"Comme vous me jugez mal en croyant
que je ne saurais pas m'abîmer dans l'affec-
tion que vous me dépeignez virile et en me
condamnant à la femme que vous supposez
être ici, que vous peignez à votre gré! Vous
avez été injuste dans bien des appréciations.
Moi, vendu à un parti pour une femme! un
homme chaste pendant un an! . . . Vous
n'y songez pas: une âme qui ne conçoit pas
la prostitution! qui regarde comme enta-
chant tout plaisir qui ne dérive pas et ne
retourne pas à l'âme! Oh! vous me devez
des réparations. Je n'ai pas eu les pensées

que vous me prêtez. J'ai horreur de tout ce qui est séduction, parce que c'est quelque chose d'étranger au sentiment vrai, pur."

This foreign, Teutonic sentimentality about the domestic relations has an influence in separating Balzac from France. Frenchmen, as a rule, do not like it, they do not respond to it: it lacks pungency (except when exaggerated into candy *à l'usage des jeunes filles*). This sentimentality goes with the rest of Balzac's wallowing, exaggerated nature. Good form frowns upon so much personal feeling, so much unrestrained emotion, as is everywhere prevalent in Balzac.

There is a note all through his novels which rarely sounds in French literature—a note of piety, purity, and belief in innocence. Imitations of this note abound. The imitation is the *aria* which almost every French author, from Bernardin de Saint-Pierre (indeed, from the author of *Aucassin et Nicolette*) down to Zola and Anatole France, feels bound to play on some magic flute, which each of them borrows for a moment from a bystander. But alas! they generally force the note, for lack of familiarity with the delicate instrument. How different are

BALZAC

the young girls of Balzac from the *ingénues* of Alfred de Musset! There is a warmth and a calm in them, a good sense, a weight, and a glowing unconsciousness which is more Dutch than French, and which the French resent. To the French temperament all this side of Balzac's art seems a little flat, a little disgusting.

And yet this power of depicting youth and goodness is the result of immense force, natural goodness and intellect. Such a picture as Balzac draws of the early life of Josephine Claes in the *Recherche de l'Absolu* can be drawn only by a man whose soul lives in the love of innocence. Balzac has the feelings of youth and the clairvoyance of later life. In his pictures of the poor and the unfortunate there is the same depth of feeling. When we reflect that this is the author who is chiefly remembered as the creator of bad characters, we get an impression of the scope of his talents.

Balzac's first grand passion was for Madame de Berny, a woman much older than himself, who had had eight children, and whom many people think was the best friend he ever had. Her death took place some time after his affair with Madame Hanska had begun, yet it seems to have smitten him with the sort of sharp grief that a child feels on learning of the death of its mother.

Both the novels and the letters show us in Balzac a man who is sentimentally constant, romantically domestic. His ambition and his sense of honour are tinged with romance. He refused money from his friends at the time he needed it most. He was determined to triumph by himself. He would not cede the manuscript of one of his novels to Prince Metternich, though the request for it was made with delicacy, because he conceived that a manuscript was a sacred personal thing which should be given only to a friend or a lover.

His letters are the most affectionate letters in existence,—always to a small circle of friends and family,—ever the same circle. I give a short paragraph which summarises a whole sheaf of these letters:

"Va! si Dieu me prête vie, j'aurai une belle place et nous serons tous heureux; rions donc encore, ma bonne sœur, la maison Balzac triomphera! Crie-le bien fort avec moi pour que la Fortune nous entende, et, pour Dieu! encore une fois ne te tourmente pas!"

## BALZAC

This cheerful courage is the prevailing mood
of his temperament. He became a notabil-
ity in 1827 with the *Chouans,* and remained
a star in Paris, especially to all foreigners
there; but these things meant little to him.
He refused to wait over a week in Berlin,
where the court society was ready to fête
him. He was bored by the heartlessness of
drawing-room life, as appears so clearly in
his books. On the other hand, he was
neither a man's man nor a sport. His club
friends were agreeable but not necessary to
him; and we must remember also that the
peculiar divisions of his day and night made
social life impossible, though they worked
in admirably with his habits of hiding from
debt.

As for those debts of which we hear so
much, they resulted from the hopefulness of
his temperament and from his weakness in
finance. This kind of man is ever being
tempted to shake off debt through speculation. He sees gold-mines everywhere. I
give the following as a sample of Balzac's
hopefulness. He has purchased a small
*pied-à-terre* at Ville d'Avray. It was called
Les Jardies.

## GREEK GENIUS

"Aussi, grace à cette circonstance, les
Jardies ne seront jamais une folie, et leur
prix un jour sera doublé. J'ai la valeur d'un
arpent, terminé au midi par une terrasse de
cent cinquante pieds et entouré de murs. Il
n'y a encore rien de planté; mais, cet au-
tomne, je compte faire de ce petit coin de
terre un Éden de plantes, de senteurs et d'ar-
bustes. A Paris et aux environs, on obtient
tout ce qu'on veut en ce genre, pourvu qu'on
ait de quoi le payer. J'aurai des magnolias
de vingt ans, des tilleuls de seize ans, de
grands peupliers, de grands bouleaux rap-
portés avec leurs mottes, du chasselas venu
dans des paniers pour être récolté dans l'an-
née. Oh! cette civilisation est admirable!
véritablement, si la paix et la prospérité pro-
gressive de ce règne continuent sous les
règnes suivants, on ne saurait prévoir à quel
degré de bien-être et de béatitude matérielle
atteindra ce bienheureux pays, surtout si les
circonstances n'entravent pas la marche de
la nature, qui l'a traité avec une si maternelle
prédilection. Aujourd'hui, mon terrain est
nu comme la main; au mois de mai prochain,
ce sera surprenant."

The sympathetic reader will have foreseen
and forewept the sequel. Within a month

the garden walls at Les Jardies fell down
because they had been built without foundations; and within two years the property
was sold and became to Balzac a memory of
pain.  He begs even his beloved Madame
Hanska never to refer to it.

The love of luxury and the passion for
bric-à-brac, which we all connect with Balzac, were peculiar, imaginative passions.
Bric-à-brac fed his mind.  It was the romance of history to him, and meant to him
the social life of past ages, the essence of
romantic association.  Cathedrals and ruined
castles spoke to him not more powerfully
than bureaux, pictures, bits of carving, and
Italian stuffs.  His *forte,* his special talent,
one of his great sources of power, lay in his
understanding of the trappings of life.  In
lodging and furnishing his characters he
makes their bedsteads and clothes, their cur-
tains, carpets, and wall-papers, speak as
eloquently as their lips.  The meaning of
furniture was one of his discoveries; he
draws orchestral voices out of it.  What
wonder, then, that such a man should value
those magnificent orchestrations of the great
costumed ages of the past?

But Balzac had no taste for luxury.  The
few objects with which he fed his fancy

were, till the close of his life, like the ancestral *bibelots* of the mandarin—things to be worshipped while he was living in small apartments and having in a cook twice a week to boil some beef, which he ate cold at every meal till her next visit. He did, it is true, commit the folly of buying and furnishing a house to receive Madame Hanska, but this was a sentimental extravagance, a mistake, a grotesque, imaginative folly, rather than an act of luxury. He seems really to have had no taste for luxury, except as a sort of revel. He enjoyed a coloured dressing-gown of an Asiatic cut, which was given him in Russia, and walked up and down in it with the glee of a child.

These things show the eccentricities of a man of genius, but show no taste for luxury. In his books there is an Oriental delight in excess, there are descriptions of feasts in which waste and delirious superflux of sensation disgust us with pleasure. There is extravagance here, bad taste, perhaps; but do not call this luxury. The luxurious man spends twenty francs on his dinner, or buys a handsome waistcoat. Balzac has not two coats to his back, but writes furiously in a monk's robe.

His burly image is engraved upon our

imaginations. Balzac the solitary, detached, prolific, indomitable creator has become one of those presiding geniuses whose busts crown the library of the mind. Volition has little to do with our acceptance of these worthies. Their names have significance for all men, because all men—even those who know nothing of them beyond the name —have been reached and influenced by them.

# IV

# LA VIE PARISIENNE

*"Il faut avoir ni foyer ni patrie pour rester à Paris."*
—Balzac.

## THE WOMEN

I BEGIN with the women, because I am
writing this essay in the hope of saving a
favourite niece, who thinks of making a
plunge into the vortex of Paris. Her im-
pulse seems to be due to an illusion that she
has artistic talents.

The clever woman who is born in America and craves excitement without having
the vigour to be emotional, finds herself in
Paris as easily as the young silk-worm, on
emerging from the egg, finds himself sitting
on a mulberry leaf and prepared to begin his
breakfast. The worm has bitten his way
through the leaf and sits on top.

The novelists have given us pictures of
the climbing American girl—pictures perhaps
too dark, yet true in the main. They show
that by the mere instinct of climbing, or the
mere passion for excitement, a certain type
of American woman finds herself in Paris.
These novels often come from the hands of

the women themselves, and show a great
mastery over one side of the subject.
They depict with unchristian gusto the
moral degeneration of the characters. They
seem to be punishing the children of their
own imaginations, as if the creatures
were their personal enemies. The general
tendency of social fiction has of late years
been towards this sort of cruelty, and
enough has never been said in extenuation
of the faults of the American heroines, or
indeed in explanation of the whole phenomenon of those wingless women who sit
crunching mulberry leaves in Paris. They
are maids who have been starved at home;
they have been bored, they have been left
unsatisfied by the social amenities of America. And from infancy they have struggled
and fought, and sought, and tasted, and
pushed blindly up until, at last, they have
reached Colombin's cakes, Louis XV decora-
tions, the titillation of refined conversation;
in short, *tous les agréments de la vie*. Here
in Paris is the elegance which they longed
for in their cradles—chairs that rest them,
sensibility that understands them, a new and
not too great excitement for each hour of
the day: the trees in the spring, the hats in
the shop windows, the latest book, the latest

## LA VIE PARISIENNE

genteel gentleman with something to say
that is full of interest (he has seen a balloon,
he knows the Swedish ambassador, he is a
complete knight and a delightful, educated,
romantic European).

There is something that Paris gives to the
American woman whose domesticity is un-
satisfactory which nothing in heaven or
earth can replace—not religion, not love,
not ambition, not care for the children of
her womb, not the memory of scenes of her
childhood, not old friends: nothing but the
feeling of beautiful Paris goes quite to the
right spot in this American female.

Of course there are differences in quality
and in the refinement of taste among these
enraptured children of Eve. The coarse-
minded and uneducated find the pang of the
poison in lace and diamonds; the refined and
educated find it in the phrases and *nuances*
of the drawing-room life. It is a fact, however, that a specific psychological relation
exists between these women and this city.
This is what makes the whole matter a fair
subject for examination and analysis, for
prayer and meditation, for uplift and re-
form, for record and historic commemora-
tion.

Surely mankind may draw some lesson

from a devout study of these acknowledged mysteries. The great thing would be to find out what happens to these pleasure-seeking females at the turning-point; that is to say, at the very moment when they reach Paris. They must, of course, do something different from what they did before reaching Paris, for Paris is the top; once Paris is reached, there is nowhere to go but down. This must cause some sort of convulsion in their silken natures. I assume, of course, that each one has got to the top of her own particular Paris, whether it be in a restaurant or in French salons. What happens when the worm reaches her limit and further climbing is positively impossible? Does she go round and round? Does she get thinner or fatter? Does she go into a doze and spin? My belief is that when she strikes her limit she begins to die. Thereafter the refinements become a habit, their pleasure-giving power of course diminishes. She is now a complete product of the American colony. Desiccation and contraction gradually reduce her to the paper-doll condition which is familiar to us all.

Another interesting study would be to determine whether a woman has ever been saved from the fate of Paris. Has a lover or a son ever plunged through the fire and brought one back alive, set her by an American fireside, interested her in her children's fate, warmed her back to such a point of vigour that the coarse blasts of American life could blow upon her soul and feed her within? The novelists have never imagined such a rescue, and the thing is probably very rare.

Still another point to be determined would be whether this Paris disease is congenital (which I rather believe), or depends upon circumstances. Given the American girl with such and such a percentage of passion, so much brains, so much education, so much money: does not the rest follow inevitably, just as the tadpole grows into a frog and not into a lion? And might not some extremely great doctor in North Adams, Massachusetts, as he examines a new-born female infant and holds the little worm to the light, wrinkle his brow, think deeply, take off his glasses, and say impressively the single word, "Paris"?

There is an innocence about these fellow-countrywomen of ours to whom this essay is dedicated, somewhat like the innocence of a man who has a paper attached to his coat-tail without being aware of it, or the inno-

cence of the drunkard, or the innocence of
the self-reliant strong man who cannot be
fooled, and whom his wife fools and manages till the audience which ought to be
amused is tempted to feel pity. They hang
like leeches on French civilisation, so visible
are they, so detached, so peculiar, so much
a class by themselves, so eccentric, so exotic,
so artificial. And yet they are of all people
in the world the most convinced that their
feet are on solid ground, that they understand life, that they know the meaning of
nationality, that they hold the secrets of the
intellect. Every breath of breeze that fans
them thinner and dries them harder brings
to them a new sensation of robustness and
succulence. Every light that makes them
look like caricatures makes them feel like
well-grounded and central personalities.

The change that comes over them when
they reach their zenith is unconscious. Death
is unconscious—and the decadence of the
spirit is always unconscious. The conscious
part of life is the awakening, the being born,
the growing, the becoming sensitive to wider
forms of truth; and exceedingly unpleasant
it generally is. One would never go to Paris
to gain this experience, though one would
willingly go there to escape from it.

## LA VIE PARISIENNE

The Psychology of Pleasure and Pain: this is the great subject which our study of the American woman in Paris leads up to. What is the injury that some pleasures do to us? What kinds of pleasure are to be looked upon askance? What element in pleasure is it that hurts the intellect? for there exists some such element. Some kinds of pleasure injure the intellect in the very moment that they seem to increase its activity,—opium, for instance, and many other drugs,—special stimulations, which give intense pleasure in specific areas of the consciousness. The most powerful that I can think of at the moment is the excitation of vanity. I had rather that a man take a dose of opium than a dose of vanity, so far as his mind is concerned. Vanity is a cutting poison that destroys portions of a man's nature, as vitriol burns flesh; and vanity is one of the intensest pleasures of which the human heart is capable. The same is true of a great rage. Indeed, the artificial stimulants which heighten an enjoyment of life, such as whiskey and tobacco, and seem to harm us in ways that medicine reaches easily, have strong rivals in those purely psychological excitements which damage us in ways that medical science cannot reach. Perhaps the

[ 299 ]

psychological effect is what does the injury in both cases.

My only point here is that there are innocent-seeming occupations which give the most thrilling joy and which do our minds the most desperate injury,—occupations that kill the very nerves of life.

These American women whom fate has thrown into a class by themselves, and whom for half a century we have been able to study as they passed through various stages of moral decay, are plainly the victims of some sort of injurious pleasure. It must be pleasure that hurts them, because they themselves confess that pleasure is their reason for living in Paris; pleasure is their aim in life, pleasure they get. This pleasure must be injurious, for behold its work!

## II

### WICKED, LOVELY PARIS

BEFORE taking up the cases of these ill-starred women, let us say a few words about Paris itself. The whole world, not America only, needs to be inoculated against the charms of that city. She has ruined generations of English people. She destroys the

[ 300 ]

## LA VIE PARISIENNE

Turk, the South American, the Russian, the West Indian, the Persian. There is something about her so free, so agreeable, so capable of satisfying the humour of everyone, so sensible, so clever, so unspoiled, so unsophisticated, that not to have seen Paris is not to have lived at all. The side streets are as interesting as the streets of little-known, remote Italian towns. The neat squares and distances are the most beautiful in the world. For a franc you get a touch of magic; it may be in a spear of asparagus, or in a glimpse of the roof of the Louvre. Paris is the Arabian Nights, we must admit it. We have all known the glamour and the joy.

The experience, however, wears thin for most people. The man with a life and a country of his own goes back to them gladly after shorter and shorter visits to Paris. He gets from Paris, perhaps, a whiff of the past, a note of his own romantic early feelings, a breath of beauty old and new. But he is content to leave. He flees it, in fact; it palls. It sends him back eager for all that it cannot give and has never given, except to Frenchmen.

Now the victims of Paris are persons who never get their second wind; they are keeled over again and again, and as fast as they stagger to their feet they are felled again by some unseen power of her charms. The lotus, the lotus! here doth it bloom indeed! The devil of the place is that it is so easy to get to. If it were Bagdad, and no railways existed, it would seduce but a few rich epicureans whom the world could well spare; but Paris takes up the ordinary London nobleman, or the New York millionaire, and it draws to its heart of loadstone the fluttering non-maternity of all countries.

For Americans Paris is merely the focal, burning point of the general attraction which Europe normally exerts upon their simple natures. We in America are children of European civilisation, and Europe is our home. Of course we are delighted at finding everything so well done, so old, so cheap, so thrilling as everything is. When an American goes to Europe he is a rustic on a visit to the metropolis. It would be a disgrace to us if we were not enchanted with the sights and sounds of the Old World. And indeed no one can complain of us in this respect. The American child, when he sees Europe, gets a new impression of his whole human inheritance.

# LA VIE PARISIENNE

## III

### THE DAMNED

THE Americans who become so bewitched with the Old World as to reside in it may be rightly divided into three classes: Vulgarians, Natural Nobles, and the Inner Temple. The Vulgarians are those who frankly like the good things of the world, and find they get more for their money in Europe than at home. The Natural Nobles are those Americans who discern in themselves a kindred natal aristocracy which binds them to Europe. They feel as if they had been changed at birth and were really European persons of family, with coats of arms, good accents, and men-servants. They cannot remember a time when they did not feel like fine ladies and gentlemen. They hold the hands of the real nobles very tightly when they meet them, and look in their eyes very lovingly. They are really long-lost brothers to dukes and kings, to barons, and to persons with old names and good manners,—indeed, to almost anyone who has the run of the great houses or small houses where the sacred society of refined and titled Europe congregates. A holy smell, as of incense, pervades the habitations of the elect in Europe; a gentle radiation of influence causes the Natural Noble from America to purr and raise his back and rub himself against the knees of the great,—yea, even against the chairs and wainscoting.

The Inner Temple consists of the intellectuals. These are people who, in the way of books and letters, pictures, small talk, and parlour education, find themselves happy in Europe and unhappy in America. They are often staunch democrats in social sympathy, but they melt before the finesse of European cultivation. Crudity is their bugbear.

It will be seen that all of these classes run into one another, and are really portions of a sort of spiral hierarchy, made up of Americans who are sensitive towards the refinements of (1) cookery, (2) social manners, and (3) æsthetic expression. The Vulgarians are the most robust of the three classes, for they proclaim the lowness of their aims, and they frankly enjoy contact with one another. They are the *tiers état,* the good *bourgeoisie* of the American Colony. These *bourgeois* are, of course, despised by the Natural Nobles, whose illusion it is that they themselves associate only with

foreigners. The Vulgarians are especially
unpleasant to them, because the Vulgarians
are in their way; the Vulgarians are a re-
proach to them, a travesty of them. The
Vulgarians make the path of the Natural
Nobles difficult in Europe in a thousand
ways. Often a Natural Noble has sisters
and brothers who are Vulgarians; for Natural Nobility is a personal sanctification, an
illumination, a grace rather than an inheritance. In this it differs from the older
European nobility, which depends upon externals. The American noble is noble by
virtue of an inner revelation.

When I was a child of about seven I was
taken to St. Cloud, and on that day the
Spirit descended upon me and I became one
of the Elect. It was in a great drawing-
room, with miles of polished parquet floor-
ing and hundreds of spindle chairs, gilded
more completely than it would be thought
possible to gild anything,—gold chairs they
looked like,—and many crystal chandeliers,
and many tall windows and many mirrors
and cheval-glasses. I was struck dumb with
delight, and I said to myself, "This is the
sort of thing that I like! It is native to me;
I have always been waiting for this! It
must be that I am a king!"

GREEK GENIUS

In this early experience of my own I seem
to see an explanation of the American Colony in Europe. From the Vulgarian to the
Inner Temple, the American Colonist in
Europe feels that he is really at home. He
is in Abraham's bosom. All the beginning
of his life was an unpleasant dream. All of
that early New York, all of that deadly Boston, *ne compte plus.*

The Inner Temple has, of course, a better
developed metaphysical consciousness than
the other two classes. The Inner Temple is
the Flower of the Bean—"the bean-flower's
boon," as Browning would say. It is the
perfect gentian of a rootless flower, and it
blossoms in the boudoir of a Spirit that lives
*in vacuo.* These intellectuals have found
their heaven, too. Why, they are as much
at home in books and in pictures as the worm
is in the chestnut.

## IV

### ABBÉS AND CUPS OF CHOCOLATE

Now I must make a digression, at the risk
of fatiguing the reader, and must tell him
that there has always existed in Europe a
whole society of critical cleverness which

LA VIE PARISIENNE

runs behind the progress of the arts like dogs
at a fair. The parlour oracle was a common character in Roman society, as one may
see in Horace. So is the man that knows
the last joke or the last news. It has always
been a game in Europe to surprise people in
the drawing-room, to give the quip, to show
oneself to be *au courant,* to take the trick
in conversation,—and, above all, to shun
crudity. This game of shunning crudity is
to-day a living part of the Roman Empire
which shines in the drawing-rooms of every
European capital, and which, by the way,
anyone can learn to play in the course of
two weeks. It is a shallow, foolish game—
a bore of a game; but the *bon-ton* has always played it, and always will. Men of
real importance who move in the *beau monde*
play it out of habit, and a whole world of
insignificant people play it because it is their
religion.

This drawing-room world of social and
æsthetic chatter draws such vitality as it has
from the deep currents of national life that
flow about it and over it. It is a fringe of
those real intellectual worlds which lie invisible in the great peoples of Europe. It is
a sort of servants' dining-hall, which implies
the existence of masters and of royal folk

[307]

somewhere else. Tolstoi shows this chatter world to us in one of its aspects, Thackeray in another, de Goncourt in another; and all of the moralists who have described it make you feel that this tavern of criticism and *bibeloterie* is a little wart or excrescence which grows on the body of Art. It is a parasite—perhaps a necessary parasite— which all healthy art supports without evil consequences.

Now the Inner Templar from America gets into this tavern of criticism and thinks he is seeing life. He finds (at first almost to his surprise) that he is holding up his end with the rest; no one resents him; he is encouraged; no one knows that he is different from the others; he does not know it himself. But the truth is that, unlike the others, he has no home, but must sit up all night when the rest have gone to their families. He has no customs, no habits, no unconscious support from a world of his own. The things he eats are not his. His very toothpick is of a foreign model, and he speaks to his valet in French. After he has talked his proper chatter about Art, he may go to a hired room to work over Art.

# LA VIE PARISIENNE

## V

### THE CREATIVE WORK OF ALIENS

A MAN who writes is like a spider who draws a web out of his stomach: the thread of his own life is revealed in the process. Art is the most personal matter in the world; and nevertheless the artist is—as we shall see in a moment—a mere embryo enclosed in society as the frog's egg is held in its place on the surface of a pond,—protected, fed, and controlled by those vital forces with which it is most immediately in contact.

As we all know, it is the early years of life that most deeply impress all men, and most seriously influence the poet and the novelist. An artist is forever telling about his earliest impressions; and the whole power of his art, which increases with age and practice, is put to illustrating the thoughts and passions of his earliest years.

Let us now recall the problems which normally occupy the minds of Americans who reside abroad. And note here that we are drifting towards the universal in these speculations, which concern themselves as

much with London as with Paris. The
dear old maids from Baltimore, New York,
and Boston who founded the American Colonies in Europe,—the Forty-niners,—were
always interested in cheap *pensions*. You
paid six francs at one place, but they would
not black the shoes there; the coffee was best
at No. 47, but you have quarrelled with No.
47 and regretted having done so. In the
course of time, when Art, and the self-consciousness of Art, began to creep into the
American Colonies in Europe, this Art was
coloured by the triviality of the life. The
Art dealt with things that might be seen by a
fly, stale things, spots and externals, the
soul-problems of the lodging-hunter and of
the tuft-hunter. There was no vigour, no
passion, no big interest in this life, or in the
reflection of this life in its works of art.

It is not merely that the literary members
of these colonies write about unimportant
things. It is that all these colonists have
nothing important to think about, and hence,
when they write, they write *chiffons*. Their
bards sing, not of arms and the man, but of
petty miseries, pimples on the face of society, mean ambitions, empty hearts. The
little blights and lichens of social life are put
under a microscope and enlarged into

hideous ugliness. And all this epidermic school of letters (which, by the way, is a peculiarly American product; no one else ever wrote in this manner before) is conducted with appalling seriousness and in pretended imitation of Balzac, and Flaubert, and I know not of whom.

Here, then, comes the revelation of the great gulf that lies between the Inner Temple and any normal intellectual life: the Inner Temple has no outer temple. It is a core without an apple. Your American novelist in London or Paris is shut into his studio with his dreams,—and he dreams of Americans abroad. And when he runs short of Americans abroad he is obliged to return to 1872 and to give pictures of Kentucky before the war. He cannot throb with the healthy emotionalism of European life; nor can he draw upon the contemporary life of his own people. His relation towards his own people has become hostile and querulous. His brain is starving for support from his fellow-men.

The great *djinn* who does the work for the artist, the slave who draws the water for the hero while he sleeps, who mows the ten acres of corn in a night,—this mysterious friend is the Unconscious. And this Unconscious is somehow a thing which other people share.  It is the block out of which we are hewn, and the pit out of which we are digged.  The Unconscious is the great umbilical cord that holds a man in touch with the universe and permits the power of the universe to reverberate through him.  How explain this phenomenon?  How make a man believe in the importance of a force which must in its very essence always remain unconscious?

These floating Americans, whose cultivation represents the wart without the body, have detached themselves from the great dynamo of life.  If one could see what was happening in the souls of these people, one would long to cut them down like suicides. What the reasons may be for this loss of power in expatriated persons we do not know.  Apparently nature speaks only through a crowd.  There must be a great many individuals who all feel alike before any one of them can say a word that is true. There is ingenuousness at the bottom of all power; a real belief that your way of thinking must prevail, because you know that everyone at bottom is like yourself,—this belief is what makes your words count.

Consider Walter Scott's way of writing,

## LA VIE PARISIENNE

or Napoleon's way of commanding. Consider a Frenchman's way of driving in a nail, or an Italian's way of eating macaroni. Consider the air with which an American rings a door-bell and then stands nonchalantly on the door-step, waiting for the door to be opened. There is a whole-hearted and headlong manner of life which betrays itself in all these activities, and which makes us see and feel that the thing in hand is important.

There are certain flowers from whose root a long filament goes out, a hairy process which is called a *biotic root*. This biotic root is an insignificant, superfluous-looking string, and often is accidentally destroyed while the flowers are being transplanted; but when this superfluous-looking root is cut the plant dies. Now the quality which the expatriated American loses is somehow due to the loss of his biotic root; but to say just what the thing is or does, whether in horticulture or in a spiritual sense, is beyond our power.

[313]

# GREEK GENIUS

## VI

### THE POOR INDIAN

THE terrible thing about Nature is that she
operates but never explains. Nature lets a
man die for lack of oxygen, but she never
says to him: "What you need, my dear fellow, is oxygen." The scientist and his labor-
atory are required to find the labels for the
poisons of the world. We see certain evil
symptoms, certain weaknesses and faint-
nesses of nature, deficiencies of energy and
dead spots; but we can never be sure that we
have properly accounted for them. If there
is any truth in my diagnosis of the heart and
brain troubles which attack Americans re-
siding in Europe, then we must look a long
way back for the causes. We must go back
to Columbus' time, and perceive that the
rush of Europeans to America and their
segregation for a few centuries on a new
soil made them peculiarly sensitive to certain
home microbes, certain drawing-room dis-
eases of Europe, from which their frontier
life had been peculiarly free. When the
Americans return to Europe the pleasures
of the intellect become to them a danger,

[314]

# LA VIE PARISIENNE

because they roll themselves in those pleasures as a cat rolls in valerian. The cult of cultivation, which is merely a becoming sort of fashionable cough to thousands of Europeans, runs straight into scarlet fever and typhoid with the American visitors. The pose of refinement, the dread of crudity, the love of *bibelots,* become, as it were, mortal sins to the long-lost American.

We must note one very interesting fact: the American who is in Europe selling steam-boilers or distributing Belgian relief, or even on some business connected with art or literature, does not show signs of this fussy sickness. He does his business and goes home. It is the man who stays in Europe in search of sensation that catches the disease.

The disease in all its forms is Nature's punishment for the vice of seeking sensation. The *dilettantes* of ancient Rome, who suffered from it, were people who wanted to draw a little more pleasure out of life than health would permit. "We are all of us too clever!" says Montaigne; "and in order to grow wise we must become dull." Now Americans have not enough reserve power to indulge in any cleverness at all, with impunity. They exhibit the rarest variety of the disease of cleverness which has ever been known, because they have lived in the wilderness till they have lost the power to take sophistication lightly. Sophistication is poison to them; they die of it, as red Indians die of whiskey.

Our only road to strength in America lies through the building up of the arts and sciences *in America,* and in an increase in the general complexity of our social and intellectual life. Your intelligent American will stand more chance of becoming a significant intelligence if he babbles in the purlieus of Hoboken than if he hobnobs with the Sorbonne. He will then be able to retain his own point of view on entering Europe, and will not drop it in the antechamber of the first European house he enters. When he goes to Europe he will go as the business man does, bringing his own thoughts, his own wares, his own aims and habits with him and feeling no false shame as to his crudity. He will not be so impressed with the importance of small things, whether they be visiting-cards or the tittle-tattle of the intellectual classes, as he is at present. He will, in fact, have a self-respecting and natural relation, instead of a

LA VIE PARISIENNE

simian and nervous relation, towards the
things of the mind in the Old World.

After all, the typical American manufacturer who comes abroad with his foolish
wife and daughters and is held up to ridicule in the novels of the Anglo- and Franco-
American literatures (this school of fiction
seems to have only one theme) is a step
nearer to true cultivation than the rest of
the characters in the books,—a step nearer
than the authors who write them; for this
manufacturer is a part of a continent and
of a tradition, a part of an unconscious
force. The other personages are dried
leaves.